Richard W. Ogden is Vice President, Manufacturing, for the Seminole Manufacturing Company in Columbus, Mississippi. A frequent contributor to trade journals and author of *Manage Your Plant for Profit and Your Promotion* (AMACOM 1978), he is also a member of the select Technical Advisory Committee of the American Apparel Manufacturers Association.

HOW TO SUCCEED
IN BUSINESS
AND MARRIAGE

Richard W. Ogden

HOW TO SUCCEED IN BUSINESS AND MARRIAGE

amacom

A division of American Management Associations

Library of Congress Cataloging in Publication Data
Ogden, Richard W.
How to succeed in business and marriage.

1. Married people—Employment.   2. Businessmen
—Family relationships.   3. Success.   I. Title.
HQ734.043   301.42′7   78-15072
ISBN 0-8144-5483-6

© 1978 AMACOM
A division of American Management Associations, New York.
All rights reserved. Printed in the United States of America.

First Printing

To my wife, Nancy

Contents

1   The Eternal Conflict—Company and Marriage   1

2   What's Important   20

3   Vagaries of Company Life—Paying the Piper   41

4   Keep the Line Open   57

5   To Move or Not to Move—and if You Do   71

6   Planning and Making the Best Use of Family Time   89

7   Proper Care and Feeding of the Other Half   105

8   Rights, Freedoms, and Responsibilities   117

9   Be Romantic   133

10   Getting the Most Out of a Company Marriage   148

1

The eternal conflict— company and marriage

FROM THE BEGINNING of time the male of the cave—or household—has worn the mantle of Provider. It's been his duty to go out and do whatever necessary to feed, clothe, and shelter his family. The woman, on the other hand, has been the Nourisher. Her duty, aside from food gathering and domestic chores, has been to feed and care for her children and to tend to and support her mate.

With the coming of the industrial age, things began to change. Perhaps the greatest change in the last century and a half has been the transition from subsistence living to a society in which just staying alive is no longer the major consideration. This has dramatically altered the traditional relationship of man and woman. The woman no longer sees her place as exclusively in the home and the man no longer considers himself the only one who should provide for the family. It is now common for both husband and wife to have employment—not to survive, but to maintain a high standard of living. And all of this is great—except for the couples who get caught up in the rat race, only to find their lives and marriages disintegrating under the pressures.

Our relative affluence affords a different sort of luxury unavailable to previous generations: married people today can question whether it's all worth it or not, whether the success, the money, the lifestyle are worth the time, effort, and the strain.

There's no question about it: marriage has become one of the great casualties of the modern world. As people move into the corporate whirl and begin the never-ending battle upward, stresses are placed on the marriage bonds with many of the ties being severed—in fact, so many that one wonders if it's inevitable. Working people are beginning to question the gain versus the loss. Does it have to be career *or* marriage? Isn't it possible to have both a successful career and a happy marriage?

The answer—a resounding yes! It's possible to have both. If you're willing to work for it, it's possible to have a career and a marriage that complement and support each other. As some have learned—and as many others are learning—a good marriage serves as a tremendous boost for a successful career, and those secure in their career can be stronger and more productive in their marriage.

This is not to say there is never any conflict between the two. Nor that there's anything easy about success in both. It does mean that a career can be combined with a marriage and that great returns will come to those who do. But first, there must be an understanding of what it's all about.

Twin Demands

To be a success in the business world takes hard work, long hours, persistent effort, and constant attention. To be a success in marriage takes hard work, long hours, persistent effort, and constant attention. Both place great demands on the individual; the problem is giving each its due and not shortchanging the other. To do this, you must understand that the demands on both sides are legitimate and that that's what causes your dilemma.

If you're ambitious in the slightest you're going to want to be promoted. That means putting a little extra effort into the job—and if you're not willing to, the next guy is. That extra effort can be translated into the one irreplaceable commodity: time. Even if you work like a beaver during normal hours, there are still going to be job demands above the norm, and what you expend then is time, irreplaceable, unstretchable, beyond human control.

Even if you're not hungry for that promotion—and it's extremely unlikely you're not—you're probably hoping to at least keep the job you have. And to keep a job requires nine to eleven hours each day, when you consider travel to and from work, lunch time, and those occasional special circumstances. This is the everyday world of making a living. We're not talking about the hotshot who blindly gives his all to the job, but about the ordinary holder of any regular job.

The same thing holds true with marriage—it creates responsibilities that put demands on your time. You don't have to be any great shakes of a husband to be subject to these demands. They simply cannot be ignored, and as a decent husband you shouldn't want to ignore them.

Any Job, Any Marriage

This is how it is for all jobs and all marriages, and you're kidding yourself if you think it would be different if you worked somewhere else or married another woman. Sure, a change could mean less demands in some areas, but there would likely be more pressures in other areas. And while some careers have more hassles than others, their rewards may differ so that it all balances out in the long run. It is imperative, then, to know what your job obligations are and the effect they can have on your marriage. Then you must take the appropriate precautions so that they do not overwhelm and/or undermine your home life.

That's where the danger lies. It's not that there are time demands in a job, but that there are so many they can suffocate the very life of your marriage. Likewise, your marriage can cripple your job performance, and paralyze you professionally.

Responsibilities to a wife and children are so great that the caring husband often feels he is not doing them justice and begins to feel guilty about it. There's the temptation to take just a little away from the job to make up for it. A little doesn't seem to make that much difference, especially in light of what it can do for the marriage. It's natural to believe that the little didn't hurt the job very much, and besides, the job really didn't allow as much time as was needed for the marriage. Why not take a little more? Where's the harm?

The harm is that little by little, more and more gets taken from work and given to the marriage, only it's still not enough. The individual wakes up to find he's fallen behind in the job advancement sweepstakes, and what's worse, despite all that's been put into the marriage at the expense of the job, he's still shorting the marriage. It's hard to understand what's happening; the marriage demands are so justifiable, so understandable, so legitimate. And so insatiable!

That's the danger in shortchanging your job for the marriage: the demands never end. They are real, and they are things that you as a husband should feel you ought to do. But there are just too many for you to ever accomplish and if you try, you not only fall short but actually cheat your job. There's no way around it. If you fail to recognize the danger of what can happen, you could very well become the victim of your own big-hearted intentions.

Remember, we're not talking about momentous things— just the small, time-consuming, dangerous little ones. Things like never using lunch time to conduct business because you always have to go home for lunch; or never going into the office early because you always have to have breakfast with the family; or never staying late and never having a business dinner and never working on Saturday, all because of your wife.

These are all laudable traits and should do much to strengthen the marriage. But there have to be limits. And the limits have to be known so you can decide where to draw the line. Job and marriage are just alike in that the more you give to one, the more that one takes and the more it demands; and this circle never ends unless you deliberately put a stop to it.

Sweet and Sour

It all comes back to you as the one who has to draw the line. And being the one in the middle, it's not always easy to see what's happening and the best way to go. There are times when all is even, but somehow both the job and marriage remain subject to a continuous series of highs and lows. During certain periods the pulls of one far outweigh the demands of the other; at other times the opposite occurs. And sometimes the two pull hard simultaneously so that you think you're going to burst open under all the pressure.

But you don't. You can and will come through these intensive pressures. What you must ensure is that you don't let extreme, temporary demands of one become longterm at the expense of the other. You can usually see what's happening, but it's easy to keep telling yourself that it will take just a little more effort and last just a little while longer. Then that extra effort and time become, for all intents and purposes, permanent and you're in trouble. By giving too much to one, you cheat the other. It doesn't take long to see the results.

Or you may shortchange for a different reason. When the going gets nasty in one place it can drive you to take refuge in the other, thus giving a disproportionate amount of time there. Everybody wants some bright spot in life and if marriage or job gets really unpleasant and the other offers solace, it's normal to lose oneself in the more agreeable arena. The individual throws himself into it wholeheartedly and the bad situation in the other gets even worse.

But solace can't always be found. Hence, when the going gets rough in either job or marriage, your performance correspondingly deteriorates in the other. Bad scenes in one lead to bad scenes in the other, souring both. It turns into a vicious cycle that's darn hard to get out of. Hurt in one area, you hurt yourself in the other. Instead of getting the support that would help, there's misery in both corners.

That's why it's crucial to keep your perspective and balance in the face of rough sledding, even if it's temporary. If job or marriage get out of kilter and you let one dominate too long, both will suffer. Since there's a very real chance of seriously damaging or destroying both, you must fight this when it happens.

It would be nice if you didn't have these unpleasant excessive demands, but neither good jobs nor successful marriages work that way. They are not independent of outside pressures and influences. No one is the sole master of his fate, and if you're going to give what you should to your job, you must respond to what is legitimately asked of you. The same holds true for your marriage. There are many demands beyond your control which you must face as part of your responsibility.

Then there are the internal factors. No human is so stable that his own emotions are always completely under control. You're going to experience highs and lows in both job and marriage just by being human. You may feel that you are the most even-tempered, unaffected individual in the world—and maybe you are—but it's doubtful that you are never subject to this being-human malady. Look at yourself objectively. Have you ever created intense pressure either at home or at work simply by doing things your own way? If you're honest the answer is yes. But so what? It's no big deal; that's the way people are and sometimes you're going to be the one in the wrong.

It's the same with your wife. She's subject to the same failings you are. Merely by living together, many ups and downs, good times and bad, are going to be experienced. Even without outside pressures, living together is itself going to create tensions of its own. That's just the way it is. This is not an excuse to throw up your hands and say, "What can I do—it's beyond control." It only means it's a fact of life that you must deal with in order to get the most out of both job and marriage.

Along with the sour times there are the sweet, sweet ones. The ones so good they are what make life worth living; those wonderful times when your business life is going great and your spouse and family are there to share and enjoy it. It's the good times, the good life, that makes you appreciate why the work and effort are so necessary. The danger is in destroying the good life by chasing it. Again, it's a question of balance. When you find that moment of moments it's natural to try to hold on to it or recapture it by concentrating on what you feel brought it to pass. But it can't be done. There has to be an end, and to try to hold it will only lead you to betray one or the other. True fulfillment and satisfaction come only when you give each turn in life its due.

Sacrifice

The question is how to give marriage and career their just due. When you consider the demands of both it's hard to see how each can be satisfied. It may not be easy but it's not impossible. It comes down to how willing you are to make the effort, how much you are willing to sacrifice of your own self, your own time, your personal desires.

Most people have a great need for closeness and togetherness with another human—the kind of intimacy that marriage can give. When this is coupled with the satisfaction of a job that's enjoyed, your cup will indeed run over. That's why it's important to do whatever is necessary to have a good marriage and to give all that is humanly possible to the job at the same time. This is the only way you will get the full measure of reward. That's why you must sacrifice as much as necessary to get the most out of both. That's why you must work to make both job and marriage complement each other.

When you think about it, the word sacrifice is both the right and wrong word all at the same time. That's because we're not talking about sacrifice but investment. An investment that will pay gigantic and life-long dividends. But, as with all investments, it won't be painless. You have to feel the pinch now and then and there may come a time when you wonder if it's worth it.

What it takes to get to the promised land is doing some things you really don't want to do, like making accommodations when your own preference is to take a completely different route. You're going to have to put your spouse's interests ahead of your own at times, catering to her wants and needs. Mostly you'll be required to give in on the little things, bending here, giving there, being inconvenienced.

There are a couple of things you need to keep in mind. The

first, and a very important one for you to remember, is that this sacrifice business is not all one-sided. We sometimes forget that our spouses are called on to do some major sacrificing of their own. When you look in the mirror you may think you're looking at the paragon of an easy-to-please, undemanding, breeze-to-live-with kind of person. The fact is, no matter who you are, you can be sure your spouse has had to compromise and sacrifice in order to stay with you.

These adjustments mean changes, new ways of doing things, a completely different mode of living. Though being married to you may be easier than being married to most, it still means sacrificing, and you'd best appreciate it. Do whatever you can to make it easier for her to live with you. Try to see what living with you means and what adjustments your wife didn't particularly want to make, maybe even shouldn't have made, but did because of your bullheadedness or blindness or desire to do the best for you.

Noticing your wife's contributions will help give you a better perspective of your own. It may help you become aware of many of her sacrifices you hadn't even noticed. You may be mighty surprised at what she's given up without fuss or muss. You can't always see that she's sacrificing when you're the recipient and she's doing it because she wants to, not because she has to.

This is another thing you must keep in mind. You will have to make sacrifices because you feel you should, not because it's demanded of you. You start seeing where you can give or give up because it's what you want to do, not because your wife is holding a hammer over your head. You'll be doing yourself a great disservice if you don't look at sacrifice in this way. If everything you do is tainted by spouse pressure, you'll soon start brooding about it, resenting it, and eventually begrudging, resisting, and then completely shutting her out. When that happens, you start cheating on the marriage, on the job, and thus on yourself. And when you stop giving, you're undermining the very goal you are after.

The great thing about giving is that it will ultimately come back to you, both in marriage and on the job. Being unable or unwilling to look at it that way will sooner or later make you come up the loser. The system works on the principle that the more of yourself you give, the more sacrifices you make, and the more of yourself you invest, the greater the return you can expect. By giving to another, by making your wife's life the best possible, you're making life the best for you, too.

It will work both ways if you will let it. Just as your rewards result from sacrificing, the same is true for your wife. For a successful marriage there has to be give and take on both sides, and for many women that's what marriage is in a nutshell. The giving of herself to her husband and family is a calling far beyond and above that of any other. To deny her own wants, to go without, to sacrifice for others, is the staff of life.

So don't start thinking you must do all of the sacrificing and giving. You probably couldn't anyway. And if you did, you'd deprive the female of fulfillment of her own by prohibiting a realization of her own self-worth. By denying her the opportunity to give of herself, you are sowing the seeds of discontent. The secret is to just let her give as much as she feels she should. This is not to say you shouldn't occasionally demand a sacrifice that she knows is right but is too timid or selfish to make on her own. Don't let selfishness that she knows is wrong destroy her only because you are not strong enough to pull her out of it. Just don't turn off her giving; you'd be doing her a great disservice.

You must also let her know that the sacrificing and giving are noticed and appreciated. Giving is a fine reward in and of itself, but even the most dedicated and loving woman has to have some kind of feedback that what she is doing is useful and valued. This doesn't mean you should bubble over effusively about every little thing that is done for you, or even that you need to voice all the gratitude you feel. Instead, let your whole attitude and being reflect your appreciation, showing you are not taking her efforts for granted. All it requires is a word here, a smile there. It's also important to know when to let her make the sacrifice and when not to let her. Sometimes she will offer or attempt to sacrifice much more than she should, and you cannot let her go beyond a certain point. But you must—and this is as vital as your own sacrificing—let her give up to that point and appreciate it for the giving it is.

There's another aspect of sacrificing in pursuit of a successful job and marriage combination. In addition to putting out for your marriage, you're going to have to sacrifice personally in order to do your best on the job. It's just like marriage—you have to do things you'd rather not and you'll be required to invest time at work you'd rather save for yourself. In short, you'll have to make many minor adjustments and some major ones.

Sacrificing on the job operates on the same principle as working to better your marriage: you're really making an investment. You must give and give fully in order to secure the full measure you have coming in return. You can't give to the job what rightfully belongs to the marriage, but to reap what each has to offer, sacrifice is the name of the game. This doesn't mean that there's nothing left for you that's all your own, that there are no more free choices. It's more like changing direction for the betterment of yourself. It's finding new avenues for fulfillment, attaining a mature understanding of what it takes to satisfy yourself, reaching a deeper realization of what's important to you.

Wanting To

It's a tall order when you stop to think about it. You're facing the twin demands of job and marriage, and from the start you know it's never easy; that you'll live through both sweet and sour times; that giving is vital to the success of each. Even when you are really sure of the rewards and benefits it's not easy to overcome the obstacles you constantly encounter. To triumph, there is one trait that's vital: you've got to want to. You must have a strong desire to do your best in both in order to have any chance for success in either.

This wanting to is not as simple as it may sound. It's easy to go through the motions of trying, of "kind of wanting to," of feeling it'd be nice to have everything that's possible in the job and marriage. But this surface desire won't bring it about because nothing that is worthwhile and enduring just happens. Sure it'd be nice, but the truth is, success does not come easily.

No matter how happily married and well-situated you think you are, you are no exception to the above rule. Take a moment to think about how important both job and marriage are to you. In your job you find a certain amount of satisfaction but not the completeness you need. Sure, you may hear about the genius or artist or scientist so wrapped up in work that everything else loses meaning, or you may see an occasional husband so involved with his wife that his job is only a livelihood. But these are the exceptions. For most, satisfaction comes from participating in both marriage and the job. Fulfillment requires hard work, intensive effort, and dedication.

If you don't understand this, you simply will not work hard enough. There's nothing automatic about making a success out of a job and marriage; it's only too easy to give a half-hearted try and then blame your failure on the circumstances. And more often than not, in the long run, giving up is not the easy way out.

You become the loser. And the next marriage won't be any different because you haven't learned anything. The only way you can succeed in both job and marriage is by sticking it out, by wanting badly to succeed. You still won't have everything the way you want it all the time. You will have problems and all sorts of ups and downs. Running or hiding or blaming won't make any difference. The troubles have to be, and that's why your desire to see things through is so important.

This strong desire, this wanting to succeed, is really nothing new for most company men, because that's the only way they've ever made any advancement on the job. The trouble with many people, and the reason that company ties have led to so many disastrous marriages, is that these astute, hard-driving, success-oriented individuals have applied themselves to the one area—the job—without realizing that the same effort is necessary for a successful marriage. Too many people let nature take its course in marriage, with both partners coming up losers.

All the excuses in the world do not make either party

blameless. A positive, enlightened approach to the marriage problem can make the difference if you want it badly enough. And the thinking, knowledgeable individual will want it, because neglect invariably comes back to haunt us. When it does, it will hurt the person on the job and in the marriage. Neglect will certainly cause at least a short-term setback, and if it's the result of not caring, or not wanting to set things right, chances are your troubles will last longer, perhaps forever.

The key to having both a good marriage and a good career is really wanting both. That's the only way to gain their full benefits; that's how to receive the unparalleled enjoyment that can come with fulfillment in both; that's the only way you'll be up to making the sacrifices required. That's when you'll begin solving the dilemmas that confront and confound you instead of giving in to them.

Of course, desire is not enough in itself. If you are not willing to take the action that will make what you want a reality, you'll be doomed to failure. But desire can provide the motivation to do what is necessary. It will be the catalyst in making you at once effective on the job and strong in your marriage. It's all up to you. If you want it badly enough, you can and will be successful in both. If you don't, you won't— and you really won't deserve to be successful.

Perfect Job, Perfect Marriage

With all this talk about hard work, sacrifice, and the fact that successful combinations of job and marriage are never easy, you might wonder if anyone ever gets there, whether there is any such thing as a perfect marriage or a perfect job. Surprisingly, the answer is yes. The secret is in knowing where perfection lies. One way of learning that is to look at what perfection is not.

The perfect marriage is never going to be a serene passage through perpetually untroubled waters. Even in the perfect marriage the partners will have some painful and difficult decisions to make with respect to each other.

There is no getting around the daily challenges, frustrations, and decisions in your marriage and work. No one is guaranteed a trouble-free life and no one has ever experienced one.

What about the old saying that the grass is always greener on the other side of the fence? No matter where you are, there's always the temptation to think that someone else has it better or easier or is getting more for less. Others appear to have it made and so would you if you just had the right job or connections or luck—or the right wife! But appearances are deceiving, so much so that no one can know what it's really like for anyone else, either on the job or at home. If you don't think that this is true, try a little experiment on your own. Cast an ear about for what people say about you. Chances are they think your situation is about as good and enviable as you think theirs is. But you know what your life is like and their conceptions do not even remotely resemble it.

It's the same when you look at someone else. What you think you see and what really is aren't necessarily the same. That other fellow may seem happily married, but that doesn't mean his marriage is trouble free. No matter how it looks on the surface the other couple has problems, too, so why waste your time envying them? Practically everyone in the world, even the happiest of people, is subject to the same demands, trials, pressures, and tribulations that you are.

The advantage happy couples have is that with all the imperfections they believe their marriages are still perfect. This is not contradictory; a perfect marriage is simply one in which both man and wife get the most out of it. The perfect marriage is a match of give and take where no one wins and no one loses, but both work together to triumph over the long pull.

It's the same with your job. If you're continually looking for a job without disappointments, you're going to be continually disappointed. There is no such animal. If you're seeking a job where you will always get your way and never be crossed, you'll be likewise disappointed. Your definition of a perfect job is sadly awry if it means nothing can ever go wrong, and the people you work with never present any problems. That kind of job is nonexistent and you're wasting your time looking for it.

But there are perfect jobs—if you understand what a perfect job is. Like the perfect marriage, the job that is perfect is loaded with flaws. Sometimes a job that is perfect for you has undesirable aspects that another does not have, but the latter job is nonetheless horribly wrong for you. The perfect job is one that allows you maximum self-development, personal enjoyment, is worth dedicating yourself to, and leaves enough time for yourself and your marriage.

There are surprisingly many jobs that fit this description, so don't be too eager to settle for a bad position. A lousy job is one you suffer with rather than grow and prosper with. In a less-than-perfect job, you yourself become less than you should be both at work and at home. You shouldn't settle for that. You shouldn't settle for a less than perfect job any more than you should settle for an unsatisfactory marriage.

This can be kind of scary to think about. What you have is sure and secure. Maybe it's not exactly what you want, and maybe it's causing you much suffering, but it's what you have! Deciding to grit your teeth and suffer through it does not relieve you of the responsibility to work for the perfect marriage, and it doesn't give you the right to vent work-related frustrations on your wife. It's up to you to decide what direction to take, but life's too short not to go after the brass rings.

Only first understand what a perfect job is and realistically appraise your current situation before embarking on a quixotic chase for something that doesn't exist. Once you know what a perfect job is it is possible to have one. Yes, it's possible to have a perfect job and a perfect marriage, and to have them at the same time. But this combination will never see the light of day unless you are willing to put in the long hours, hard work, and constant effort that is required. That's a fact of life that is inescapable: the only way to have success in a job or marriage is through total, personal commitment.

Why Bother?

If success in marriage and business is so hard to come by, if it means unceasing and unrelenting demands, you must be asking yourself, why go through the bother? Obviously, in this day and age there are many ways to cop out. You may not wind up with as much as you possibly could, but there are sure to be less hassle and less bother. You can get by, making a living, be gainfully employed, and have a "meaningful" relationship without killing yourself. So why not? Why not take it easy on the job and just live with someone while the good times last and then move on to someone else?

Indeed, there seem to be plenty of people doing this. They're not giving much and they are taking what they can. They know it and the company also probably knows it, but doesn't really seem to mind. Their work borders on second rate, and at times is sloppy. They never make any extra effort, never stay late, and don't seem to care whether they're doing the right thing or not. Their habits are the same away from the job. More and more people are living together without getting married, and doing it openly, with no apologies and without ties or responsibilities. Then when the relationship ends they look for someone else to start up with all over again.

And there are others who follow the same pattern even though they have gone through the trouble of a formal wedding ceremony. It doesn't seem to mean all that much to them, they live together only until they get tired of it. Then, still friends, they decide they've had enough—it's time to go their separate ways with no remorse.

If it's all so easy, why don't you do it too? This brings us back again to the basic question, Why bother in the first place? Well, for one very important reason, the one who is losing is you. That's what it all boils down to. If you don't give your all to the job and if you're not willing to put 100 percent into the marriage, you won't get the full return and satisfaction that is possible. When you cheat you're really cheating on yourself. Like the maxim says, you only get out what you put in. If you're not willing to put all of yourself into your job and your marriage, if you're not willing to go that extra step, you not only won't get what you could have coming, you won't deserve it.

The world owes you nothing and when you try to shortcut your way to success, you end up emotionally impoverished.

Consider the job first. In our modern world we are often in such pursuit of leisure that we tend to forget how satisfying and fulfilling hard work can be. It can bring much more than monetary and material rewards, although these are important too. It can be the satisfaction of a job well done, of the fact that you're contributing, that you are a vital part of a successful company, that you are productive. But a job can give fulfillment only if you give it your all.

But as important, vital, and necessary as this part of your life is, it's not enough in and of itself. Though personal accomplishments in the work arena can be great, they pale if you have no one to share your satisfactions with. From the beginning, man has been a social animal with a great need for other humans, a great need to share triumphs and losses, to give as well as take; to belong and have someone belong to him, to love and be loved in a special, lasting way. Man, every man, needs that unique relationship with that one woman who will soar to the heights with him and plunge to the depths with him.

That's what life's all about, and more and more of the people who do get to the top freely admit that what made it all worthwhile was having the family there to share it with. Without the family nothing they had accomplished in the world of business would have amounted to anything. Conversely, one after another of those who gave up on their marriage only to advance their careers found their executive status and all the material gain empty. No matter what was accomplished, it was never enough. The man who hungered to build the biggest bridge did—and felt disappointed afterwards. Those who seek nothing but the biggest and the best will never find it. It's the children, your wife, who make it worthwhile.

Material things are never enough in themselves. Life should be more, can be more, has to be more, and will be more if you have that special someone to go the route with. With all of the ups and downs, the joys and heartaches, it's this experiencing together, making a commitment to each other, that brings out the true meaning of life. And the time to start thinking about and making that commitment is now.

You may think you're young and there's plenty of time, and

you're not really sure this woman is the one you want to give your all to. Well, it's probably later than you think, so you'd better consider it now. Plenty of people have thought they had much time left only to realize one sad day that time had passed them by. As you get older time passes by not arithmetically, but geometrically, with a speed that's unbelievable until it's experienced. Don't think you have any security in time. Don't wait for the commitment that will sustain you through life. You'll wind up the loser.

Besides all of this, there are many practical reasons for being conventional in marriage and conscientious on the job. There's the morality of the company you're working for. It may seem like the high-lifers and lazies-on-the-job are doing all right, but their day is guaranteed to be short. The people who run corporations usually got there through hard work and they are not about to turn over what they've strived so hard to create to people too lazy to contribute. And they're sticky about the morals of others within the company. Even when their own ethics are suspect they expect those in the ranks to tow the line with at least a public display of morals compatible with those of the corporation.

Then there is the question of stability. If a person is not willing to make a family commitment, if that person is just looking for the easy times, how much loyalty will he really have to the company? Why invest time and money training and developing someone who is liable to take off on a whim or when the going gets a little rough? Too risky, much too risky. There may not be termination, but there won't be any rapid promotions either.

And there's company perpetuity. The powers that be in any company can understand and even condone the free wheeling of youth, especially among those who generally observe the rules. Having sown their wild oats, they will eventually settle down to a respectable way of family and company life. But what of those who show by their actions that they do not believe in marriage? If they can't be counted on to participate in such a basic institution as that, how can they be relied on to uphold and maintain the traditions of the company? In many cases they can't or simply won't be trusted. That's why being married, or at least planning to someday, is basic to the launching of a successful corporate career.

There are also practical personal considerations that dictate marriage as the way to go. Consider peer pressure. After one reaches a certain age most of the people one associates with are married. It's still the "natural" thing to do and even when those who just live together may appear to be accepted, it's not always quite so easily done in real life.

These, then, are two very compelling reasons for marriage: to solidify your position in a company, and to bolster your status among peers. Protest as you will, these are heavy, significant factors.

But the true reason, the overwhelmingly most important reason to get married is that it *is* the natural thing to do. In spite of today's easy sex, and some of the tenets of women's liberation, the gay movement, and the whole spectrum of modern morality, most people feel the need to be married. They want it so much that the vast majority of those divorced seek yet another marriage. *It's the natural thing to do.*

There are many, many reasons why it's good to be married. You've almost certainly experienced some or most of them yourself. Here are just a few:

—It is nicer to have someone to come home to. Solitude is great until that's all one can expect to experience night after night. It doesn't take long to get lonely, and there's little to be said about eating meal after meal alone.

—People need to know someone cares about them. Someone who cares enough to sign on the dotted line, "until death do us part."

—People need to share. They want to share their hopes, their dreams, their triumphs, their disappointments, their sorrows, their failures with someone they know cares.

—Having children. There are few people who do not have some yearning for children of their own.

—Maintaining tradition. Our parents were married, as were our grandparents, uncles, aunts, relatives, and the parents of childhood friends. Most of us develop a powerful urge to do as our childhood role models did.

—To satisfy unique personal needs. Whatever these may

be, they are real and so important that many are willing to try, try again.

Thus, if marriage is to be, and the irrefutable evidence is that it is, it's logical to work to make the one you now have a success. Not all will survive, despite great effort, but most can, with enough hard work. The kind of return that comes from a good marriage is worth whatever it takes to get it and hold it together.

2

What's important

HAVE YOU EVER THOUGHT about what you really want out of life? Have you gone so far as to sit down and deeply consider it? Have you ever taken an honest look at where you are right now, where your path is leading you, and why you're letting it take you there?

It's so easy to work and slave and get caught up in the rat race of getting ahead, in the running, working, fighting, clawing, and scratching without really knowing why. You probably have some vague idea of success, a vision of money and happiness that will come if you press ever upward and onward. Many of us unwittingly get caught on this treadmill of relentlessly pursuing more and more and more.

The race becomes so absorbing that we often don't know what it is we're chasing. It becomes a race without a finish line. We become so wrapped up in today that we have little concern for tomorrow and at the same time lack a real understanding of today. When that happens, we're in deep trouble. Deep trouble because we've become too busy to get out of life what it has to offer. If your idea of success is without shape, how can you ever find it?

If you've never thought about it, or if it's been so long you've forgotten what you decided, it's time right now to stop and take a cold, hard look at where you are and where you want to go. Then look a little deeper to decide if that's what you *really* want or if it's just some foggy idea of what you think success is all about. It's not going to be easy. You have to make a full, honest appraisal of yourself as you've never done before. You must be willing to face facts about yourself without the defensive delusions everyone has a tendency to hang on to. You must strip the veneer of wishful thinking about what you'd like to be and concentrate on what you are.

This may be painful because you're seeing yourself in a way you probably never felt you had to before. You may even have avoided self-analysis fearing you'd come up short. This should no longer be an issue. No matter at what stage in life or marriage or job you now are, it's time to take honest stock of where you are, where you are likely to end up, and where deep down you want to be. This first step—to be completely honest with yourself—may be the hardest but it's absolutely necessary. You can lie to other people perhaps, but never ever lie to yourself.

Initially you should analyze as if in a vacuum, without worrying about anyone else. Later, of course, you will want to involve your wife, and it's vital that you do, but first you need to get your own values lined up and go from there. And don't think you're going to get it done in one afternoon. The effort it takes to do it right is too much for one sitting and if you don't want to make it meaningful and thorough, why bother? Let's face it, we're the difference between a meaningful life and a fruitless life.

There is an easy, pleasurable way to get into your probe of what you really want out of life. Sit back, relax, and start day-dreaming. Dream about what you'd like to be, about anything that strikes your fancy, writing it all down, even the most fanciful. Don't worry about order and cohesion; if you want, you can edit it later. Just let your wishes run wild without regard to how attainable or rational they might be. Cover all phases of your life—your job, your marriage, your secret world—everything you've always been attracted to or wanted to be a part of. It's very important that you make a complete list because this can be the start of a useful guide on how you're going to live your life.

After you've taken the time to compile a thorough list, start grouping similar items together. Make rough groupings of general categories such as job, family, marriage, and self. Then start sifting. Throw out those that are clearly pie in the sky. Cross out those you don't really expect to take place or don't mean that much to you. The refining process might require going through the list many times, but do it until you are satisfied that what is left is the bedrock of what you really want out of life.

Once you've combed your list as thoroughly as you can, start comparing categories. Look for items that are compatible and go together and use these as the start of yet another list, the master list. Find the choices in each category that may not be compatible with those in other categories—so incompatible that they even fight with each other. See if there are any goals which, if pursued, would mean having to slight or ignore another goal. See whether all that you think you want—all that you consider vitally important—is possible in light of everything else you want. An objective look will probably tell you that everything is not possible, so before you put any of these items on the master list, you must do some soul-searching to narrow them down. Sort out things that seemed compatible on the surface but really are not. This is the moment of truth when you must decide once and for all what is really important to you.

When this master list is completed, look at it not so much from the standpoint of how to get where you want to go, although that too is extremely important, but in terms of once you are there, what you will have. Equally important is the question of what you will have lost in getting there. This is where you must decide what kind of trade-offs you'll have to make in life to get as much out of it as you want. No one is immune from these basic choices; no one, absolutely no one, has ever gotten everything he wanted out of life. But without this understanding of what's important to you, there's no way you can come close. Only when you start comparing and throwing out some very dear choices do you begin to understand what is really important to you now and for the long run.

And this first analysis doesn't end the process. You must periodically review the important items to keep them fresh and pertinent. Time does strange and often wonderful things with human values; as you develop and grow they can change drastically. Your ambition may be tempered as you gain insight into the cost of gaining it. Your whole scheme of life can be altered sharply as you attain certain objectives and see firsthand whether they were worth the effort and sacrifice. Your perspective as to what is important can also change as you get older. Thus, this questioning and reaffirming of what's really important is a never-ending process. You must continue the process so that you do not get caught in a bind of your own making, having failed to take stock of changes.

Establishing priorities is no guarantee of a happy life, but it does give you something to measure your life against, a source of constancy that can help you to appraise and bring about change. Without this sense of direction your total being will inevitably amount to less than it could be, simply because of events and circumstances which wait for no man. Too many people do not realize this until their life has literally passed them by and it's too late to get all that job and marriage had to offer. It's a sad day when the individual realizes what has happened and can only wonder why and how. Don't let that tragic day dawn for you.

Your Ambition

In large measure, determining what's important depends on what your ambitions are. What you want to do and what you are doing at the moment are probably two entirely different things. It's possible that you're content where you are and that your ambition is to do only as well as you can in your present position. There's nothing wrong with that. But it's also possible that you want considerably more than you now have in terms of responsibility, money, and prestige.

Some people will never be satisfied until they are at the

absolute top, regardless of what the top is and what price they have to pay to get there. Others want to get to the top too but they don't want to pay the exacting price it takes or do not understand what that price is. They want and have "ambition," but feel that their rise is automatic, given their natural talents. They want to go very high, but on their own terms, taking the easy way. They are willing to work hard, but only according to their own rules, rather than more realistic demands.

There are others who are satisfied to let events take them wherever they will. They may want to do well and go far but do not believe they really have any influence over how far. They go along and take whatever is given, hoping things will work out all right.

And there's the great majority who kid themselves into thinking they are on the way toward fulfilling an ambition, but are gradually losing steam, letting events dictate their path. They started out as a house afire, full of vim and vigor and vitality, but somewhere along the way forgot what it was all about and where they were going. They wake up one morning and find that their youthful assurance of greatness has not come to pass and probably never will. Most are surprised to find that this has happened and can't for the life of themselves figure out what went wrong. It's a sad day but one that comes to most of us, and is almost certain to come to those who do not have a clear picture of where they want to go and what it takes to get there.

Whatever your situation, your ambition and your pursuit of it is a definite factor in your marriage. That's why you must look right now at your marriage and goals and see how each fits into your ultimate plan. Unfortunately, it is all too often taken for granted that the two are naturally compatible. This is not necessarily true. Your marriage and your ambition may not be compatible at all, because what you want from one will take away from the other.

As you develop professionally, you may not develop maritally. Your ambition may put an unnecessary strain on your wife because she doesn't understand where you're trying to go and what you have to do to get there. You may shut off her support because she does not know where she fits in, what's expected of her, or how much of the load she has to carry herself.

Or, and this is most significant, you may be chasing something you do not want. It may be a case of mistaken dreams, false ambition. In your youth it is easy to believe you want something when that really isn't what would make you happy. Deluding yourself that glitter is substance, you can end up with severe marital problems you didn't have to have. It's all too easy for ambition to be vague. For many of us there is no specific goal, just a yearning to go higher and higher until the top, whatever that is, is reached. In this blind pursuit—and an unattainable shot for most—we often take for granted that our spouses understand, and if they don't, well, they should support us automatically anyway.

But very few spouses can identify with only a vague idea of where their mates are going. And as hard as it is to admit, one's wife can often see more clearly than he can where he is going to fall short. The wife can refuse to be swept along in a "must" situation because from her perspective, she can see that it's not really urgent at all. She can predict that the family and marriage will suffer, but that the ambition will not be fruitful.

That's hard to take. Here, something seems genuinely necessary to you, but your wife disagrees and refuses to go along. You're torn, frustrated, and probably angry. Then when the emotion fades, you realize she was right.

One of the great problems that comes up in many marriages is that wives can be too brutally honest about their opinions of their husbands. Living so close day in and day out, there aren't many illusions that last for long. Your wife's opinion can be shattering if you're not prepared to hear the truth, if you have deluded yourself about what you really are.

But it's also possible to be more successful than your spouse realizes. The very proximity makes you more vulnerable at home. Some real accomplishment that you mention or even brag about might be downgraded at home because it is not understood or in some way takes away from the marriage. Instead of the praise and appreciation that is your due there is derision, and the significance of your work is lost on your mate.

That's why it's important for you both to know your goals. If you don't know where you want to go and what is necessary to get there, there's no way you can establish the necessary priorities. There's no way you can tell your wife how to give you the needed support. She won't understand what's expected from her or what you expect to have to do yourself.

The only way to get what you want is to consider your marriage and future objectively. Does what you have today fit into your overall plan? Can your marriage take the stress and demands of what must be done if you are going to get there? What must you do to develop the marriage so that it will be what you want when you finally do arrive? Can you envision your mate growing along with you?

These are not idle questions. Ignoring them is one reason so many wives become corporate casualties. An individual can become so obsessed with his ambition that he forgets the ramifications for his spouse once it's gotten or he's well on the road toward attaining it. It's easy to forget that dreams are not always shared. It's easy to forget that your wife may not be prepared for or even want a place at the top. It's easy to forget how demanding it can be to support your climb. And it's easy to forget to include your wife, who consequently gets left behind.

Be that as it may, many couples grow together, prosper together, and triumph together because they know each other well and work together. A man and woman can be very effective as a team and have a strong marriage if both know what they are after and work toward that end. And together, some re-evaluate these career goals and conclude it's not worth the price they would have to pay from the standpoint of their marriage and family. Having evaluated all factors, they turn away from blind ambition or temper their goals to fit their real wants. They mutually and wisely decide to use their talents and efforts somewhere else.

But sadly, many others come up short both professionally and maritally. They never stop to look at where they are heading in either sphere. They are content to drift and take whatever comes along, rationalizing when necessary, never in command of their lives. They chase a fantasy on the job that can never be, and lose what could have been in marriage. There comes a sudden realization that the world has passed them by. They then have a desperate need to turn homeward, but when they try to, they find it's not there any more.

You can prevent this only if you are honest about where you are now, where you really want to go, and where you are actually going under the status quo. For you, is it a plausible ambition or just a dream? Do you understand the demands that fall on you personally and those that your spouse must bear up under in order to support your ambition? Have you included your wife in your calculations? Have you really considered if it is worth it? Ambition is usually thought of as it relates to one's profession. Perhaps a better way to view it is in terms of total living, the complete life. You should consider everything including your job, marriage, and true self-satisfaction. Only in this way can you come to grips with the potential conflicts and make hard, realistic decisions as to what to do.

Her Ambition

The days of the wife waiting silently and patiently in the wings are long gone, and that's something else you must consider. It used to be that the husband was the one with or without ambition and if the wife had any, she expected to fulfill it through him. She may have had to push to get him to the heights she wanted, but the man was the one to get there and the woman just went along.

That's not so any more. Women have come to expect development of their own. Some women pursue a career while married but without the burden of children. Others feel they can handle both, while still others have their eye on the day when the kids are gone and their full energies can be focused on their second career.

There are still many who choose not to have any career outside the family and married life. They are fulfilled and content with their lot, a feeling engendered by the fact that the decision to stay home was theirs. With this independence, wives are coming to believe that they should also have a voice in helping the husband decide what his career objective should be. We have gone beyond the days when women would only assist in whatever the husband decided to do. Today they insist on the right to speak up and to participate in their husband's career selection.

So, in defining your own ambition, you must take into consideration your wife's. What does she want from life and from you? What are her long-range goals for herself, for you, and the children? How does your ambition fit with hers? Are there any possible conflicts? Does she understand what you're after and where you want to go? There may very well be differences that can affect your plans. Not that you'll necessarily change where you want to go, but you may want to alter your approach in getting there. Certainly you can't substitute her plans for yours, but her thoughts and values are very important factors.

It's only fair. You selected a mate who was better educated and more enlightened than women of yesteryear. You can't expect her to hide her own light under your bushel. She's of a time when gender has lost its power as an indicator of ability or lack of it, and no vocations are held sacred. Even if she's at an age you consider beyond the modern generation, she has no doubt been affected by the "now" thinking.

Despite the feminist movement there are many women who still find joy, comfort, and satisfaction in homemaking and raising a family. But when the children are on their own, the women want some outside action, too. They are no longer content to simply pass the time. They're still willing to help their husbands, but not as a substitute for their own ambition. It's time for themselves. They see no reason to quietly wither away, and they are not going to.

When evaluating your marriage, then, you cannot only regard the status quo. You cannot look at your goals in the context of what you alone want. You must consider your wife—her wants, her desires, her ambitions. There will probably be no conflict, but you simply cannot afford any surprises. It would be terrible if you're coasting along with one idea of your wife's dream and it turns out to be something entirely different. You don't want to build your future with her as the bedrock, only to find her support has turned to quicksand.

And there's always the possibility of the late bloomer. Your wife has been content to stay home and has had no outside ambition. But with the family gone and time on her hands, all of a sudden she discovers that she is talented in her own right; that she can go her own way and find her own destiny. In this case, help her make sure she knows where she's going. When her separate path begins to emerge you must evaluate it in terms of what it will do for her and for you. But above all remember that you cannot and should not try to keep her buried at home. You shouldn't even want to. How can you expect her to keep pace with you if you don't let her? Don't throw her out into the cold world if she doesn't want to go, but if she does, help all you can in her search to find herself.

This should be a vital part of your marriage—each helping the other find what's wanted and needed. There should be blending of career goals so that they do not compete, one pulling against the other, and both suffering as a result.

There should be no jealousy or false pride. If she succeeds it's to your credit too. Encourage her to be as good or better than you in her own work. If there is a conflict, talk it over and work it out. Let her know you're on her side all the way, so if she has to pull in her horns a little she'll do so willingly. And don't you be afraid to bend some if it will help her. Part of your marital responsibility is to help your wife find happiness on her own terms. It can strengthen your marriage if you realize she has ability and ambition of her own and you should count among your proudest moments the attainment of her dream.

Marriage Goals

Now that you've looked at what's important to you, analyzed your own ambition and found a deeper understanding of your wife's, it's time to establish some definite goals for your marriage. It's time to set down in black and white what the two of you are working toward.

You probably already know the importance of goal setting in the business world, where companies without specific targets have a tendency to float along while those that have goals, something to zero in on, press ahead on a successful path.

It's the same in marriage. The only way you can realize the full potential of your marriage is to know what your goals are. In your thinking on what's most important, you should have arrived at some pretty solid ideas of what marriage means to you and what you want out of it. Your wife should have done the same, and though it's possible your lists differed, you both undoubtedly have many wants in common. These can serve excellently as a start in determining your marriage goals.

Take it from there. Sit down with your lists and look at what your wife says she wants out of life and what you say you want. Take the things you agree on and set them aside as the start of your marriage goals. Then turn to the ones that seem to be incompatible and compare the lists side by side while she does the same. A very important proviso: do it with an open mind.

The only way it will work is if you understand that there is nothing sacred about your list and that hers is not intended to slight or offend yours. Hopefully she will feel the same way. If you run into some basic disagreement that threatens to torpedo the entire project, don't let it. If either of you gets overly sensitive and angry words start to fly you're going to be hard pressed to accomplish what you want.

This undertaking must be done in a climate of cooperation and closeness. Your own attitude is a major factor, so start there. Do your best to set the right tone. After all, this whole thing was begun on your initiative, and you may well be faced with some skepticism by your beloved, especially if you're trying to get her to see that if you don't do something, your marriage could be in deep trouble.

Begin with an open mind and the conviction that the time and effort you've expended so far have been groundwork for what follows. If you don't have an open mind yourself, you haven't captured the spirit, and there's no way you can expect your wife to, either. Besides, it's to your advantage to have an open mind because no one can think of every possibility. If you pursue common goals with a strong desire and an open heart you will quickly see that the apparent differences are not so drastic after all. Even though you are married to one another, each of you is a separate human being who has grown, developed, and matured independently of the other. This is a truth that you will never escape and one you shouldn't want to. Marriage creates an entirely new entity where the whole equals more than the parts taken separately. By working and planning together you set goals that are meaningful throughout life; goals that will encourage and even demand a commitment from each of you. And with those goals, you can further strengthen and contribute to the well-being of your marriage, your children, and each other.

On the other hand, if you can't reach an agreement, you're in trouble. It may not be disastrous, especially since you were able to go so far as to sit down together and talk, and the difference may not be irreconcilable. Still, it's serious enough to merit some intensive analysis. Now is the time to see if you can improve the situation.

If there is a danger of losing the marriage, then you have no time to waste. Don't be afraid of what you'll find, because there can be no cure if you don't admit there is a problem. The only way to surmount and overcome your differences is to get them out into the open. If you don't you'll never find a solution and the problems will simmer and fester until they blow the marriage apart. You need to face that prospect squarely. Look at the alternatives and decide the best way to go. But in so doing, look to your heart to see if a break is inevitable or if you just don't want to bother with the effort of reviving a sagging marriage.

Once you set goals for your marriage it's time to start working together to attain them. Knowing what the goals are is good, but just knowing won't make them happen. You've got to work to achieve them. By struggling together to figure out what your marriage goals are, you have already taken a giant step in strengthening your marriage. You have laid the important groundwork. It's a great start if you are willing to follow through in achieving those goals.

You must also periodically review those goals with and without your wife to determine whether you are still progressing toward them and if they are still what you want. As you grow and develop in marriage, your experiences may prompt new ideas of what marriage can do and what you want out of it. Set aside some time to see if what first seemed important still is. By taking the time and making the effort to establish goals for your marriage, you set the stage for gaining the maximum long-term return for you and your wife. It still won't be easy but matrimonial goals can make marriage more meaningful and productive for both of you.

Children

What mixed blessings, children! They generate so many of the joys, sorrows, highs, lows, thrills, disappointments, contentments, dissatisfactions, fulfillments, and heartaches of marriage. Though some couples choose to be childless, over the long run not very many will. Marriage and children go together, a condition that most people find desirable.

But attitudes about children and their place in the family have drastically changed in recent times, and the demands and strains of modern society require parents to have a rational as well as emotional approach to family. Gone are the days when large numbers of children were needed to help support the family, either by working the land or bringing in additional income. Gone are the days of excessively high infant mortality. Gone are the days when birth control was a hit-or-miss proposition, either because of ignorance, religious beliefs, or lack of contraception. Today virtually every American couple at least has the means to determine not only the number of children they will have but also when they will arrive. Planned parenthood reigns today because whether it's admitted or not, almost every couple is using at least some kind of birth control.

And this is as it should be. Couples should plan their families. The problem is that most planning to date has been primarily with regard to numbers. Very few couples take the long-range view on what they are going to do once they have them. Many children have been victims of marriages that have no direction of their own, and have no plan or thought for the raising of children either. The kids are wanted—they are loved, maybe even worshipped—but they end up with the short end of the stick because their parents haven't really thought about or agreed on what's best for them. Mom and dad have provided sustenance and a home and care and love, but as important as these are, they're not enough. Children need much, much more, the more that comes from you as a parent carefully thinking about the best way to raise them.

Children are too precious to leave their upbringing to chance. Don't put off for next year thoughts on how best to raise yours. It's especially urgent if you already have children who are well on their way to adulthood. If that's the case and you and your wife have never seriously discussed your philosophy of raising kids, you've no time to lose.

In your lists of what's important, you and your wife probably gave children and their well-being high priority. Now is the time to figure out how to get them where you want, what's necessary for you as a parent to properly raise them. It's a difficult job but it can be much easier if you and your wife agree on basic ideas and share a common philosophy.

The first thing to remember is that children are people too. They start very early developing personalities of their own, which grow more individualistic with age. This is easy to forget if you only think of them as flesh of your flesh and light of your life; but it is true nonetheless. Your children are individuals in their own right. They are not miniature reproductions of you or your wife. They have many of your characteristics and there are many similarities, but they are not you incarnate. They have different intelligence, experiences, and sets of emotions. And while this is very basic, it is often ignored or overlooked by parents. That's something you can't afford to do when designing your game plan for raising them.

As youngsters, they are susceptible to the influences of the most dominant forces around, which from the start are the parents. From the beginning they learn from parents, imitating and emulating them, setting their patterns of living by what they see at home. They will react to their parents' example one way or the other, positively or negatively, and that's why it's critical to know and agree on how you want to raise them.

Two things which every child needs are love and firm guidance. Those who feel children can do whatever they want and still turn out as they should are sadly mistaken. They are literally begging their parental responsibilities. The growing child lacks the experience to make important decisions, and if left alone by misguided parents to do so, he or she is bound to make some bad mistakes. Every child needs to feel the interest that comes from deep parental love, and guidance and discipline are ways of expressing that love.

Discipline is a key word. It's vitally important for a child that parents agree on what kind of and how much discipline they will use so that they do not work against each other to the detriment of the child. It doesn't mean that both should carry the strap—virtually gone and rightly so—but there are other kinds of discipline that occasionally must be used. Don't forget, however, that as necessary as discipline is, a very important part of it is forgiveness. You can't hold a grudge against your child without dire consequences. You and your wife need to agree on how to instruct the youngster and how to administer discipline, but especially on how to let the child back in your good graces.

The child has a very real need of discipline because it is a prime source of comfort when combined with a full measure of love. Parents who do not perceive this or who choose to ignore it do a great disservice to their offspring. The child knows, in its heart when the reason for discipline is love, and he or she also knows when lack of discipline is lack of love.

Another part of parenthood you must acknowledge is that as parents you are distinct and separate from your children. You and your wife do not have the luxury of "growing up" with them. You cannot be buddies with them to the extent that you ignore the differences and responsibilities inherent in your being the parent. Nor can you relive your lives through your children, and you shouldn't try. You must, and this is important, let your children follow their own callings no matter how different from your own. If you were an athlete but your pride and joy, your number one son, wants to be a musician or poet, so be it. It's his life and you must let him live it. He still needs your support and you and your wife must agree to supply that support—but as parents and not as buddies reliving your dreams through him.

Together you and your wife must decide what kind of future you want to prepare your children for. While you cannot and should not map it out precisely, you can provide a climate that is conducive to your children's thinking the way you feel they should. If you expect a high standard of morality from them, you must set one at home. If you don't want them to abuse alcohol or drugs, you must exemplify your feelings by action. In all areas it is up to you and your wife to develop and mold the children to the best of your ability, but it's impossible if the two of you do not agree on where you should be leading them and how.

Now is the time to take that hard look at what you are as parents, to evaluate what you have done and where your approach now is leading. It's time again for that brutal honesty, to yourself and to each other, if you are ever going to fulfill your obligations as parents. The rewards of parenthood are well beyond any measurable calculation but they only come to those who realize their responsibilities and do the work required in being good ones.

You'll never spoil children with too much love, but you sure can hurt them if you are unwilling to make a total commitment to parenthood. If you do not make provisions for doing right by them now, the day will arrive when you come up short, and on that day it will be too late to recapture what you have needlessly thrown away.

Money

Another prime consideration in the life of all married couples is money. Study after study shows that the most prevalent and recurring problems in marriages ultimately get down to money. Either there's not enough of it, or it's the pursuit of, dispensation of, or, in rare cases, too much of, money. There's no way around it—money is a problem.

For most executives, the chief concern is maintaining or reaching a certain high standard of living. It has nothing to do with basics such as food, shelter, and clothing. Company people usually live far beyond subsistence levels, although it's hard sometimes for them to appreciate this. That's because the standard of what's acceptable has changed so dramatically in the last several years. Countless items that were formerly considered luxuries are today taken for granted. It's one thing to harken back to the old days when your folks scrimped, saved, and did without, but it is increasingly difficult to do that today. Even when you're not trying to keep up with the Joneses you can get caught in a financial squeeze just maintaining a minimum standard of living.

Although we may not be talking about strict necessities, we really are in the sense that they've become the accepted norm. Take the automobile. Not long ago the second car was the mark of true prosperity. That's not so today, as we have become a mobile society that no longer has access to neighborhood jobs, shops, and schools. Most couples have more than one car because they must, and many with teenagers of driving age have more than two cars. Not because they are rich or are spoiling the kids, but because in this society an extra car is necessary.

It's the same with the location of your home. Sure, you can find comparatively low-cost housing, but in what kind of neighborhood? You want to live among and raise your children with contemporaries, people with similar tastes, interests, and income. It has nothing to do with snobbishness or racism; you naturally want to be around those you identify with. But this is a problem. Frequently your neighbors seem to be doing better and better, and the local standard of living appears to be steadily rising. You're not in the race to keep up, but it's hard not to when everyone you know is doing so much more, has so much more.

It's baffling. Expenses seem to outrun income significantly, even when you're making good money and not living extravagantly. The money just doesn't last and it's a real dilemma, with increasing costs hitting you from all sides. Your disposable income gets to be less and less because of things beyond your control, such as taxes, utilities, food, and clothes. It seems like the better you live the less you have to live with, and it's not long before you've become stretched very thin.

It's nothing you intended, and maybe you even tried to guard against it, but the result is that you're overextended financially and it's hard to see which way to go. Your nerves get strained and you can't talk to anyone without snapping. The smallest purchase becomes a point of controversy, and it takes very little to spark an ill-tempered argument between you and your wife. And it all can be traced back to the never-ending money pressures faced by every married couple.

This is a problem of such consequence that you and your wife must face it together or run the risk of letting it ruin your marriage. Unless you're one of those rare people with unlimited resources, you will simply not have enough income to satisfy all of your desires. Only by careful managing and budgeting will you be able to stretch your pay to cover most—but not all—of the material goodies you seek.

But that's a lot easier said than done, as you undoubtedly already know. There are so many legitimate demands for your bankroll that it seems impossible to turn down any even when you know you can't afford them. Living extravagantly indeed! You're not leading the pack; in fact it often seems you're trailing everyone, and it's become increasingly difficult to hold your own.

That's why you and your wife need an understanding of exactly what kind of income you have to work with. Together you must establish priorities of where you want your money to go, because it's going to require both of you working together to do it right. Too often one of the married partners is the "money watcher" while the other goes merrily along, spending the former into ulcerhood.

It's never been easy, but in the past people could survive by finally drawing the line and temporarily tightening their belts. But that's much harder to do today because the costs of so many basics are way out of line. The underlying, continuing expenses are so great today that it's difficult to cut them. Whether you are overextended or not, they keep coming.

Another complication, and a particularly dangerous one, is the availability of credit and the abuse of it. It's so easy and so tempting to buy something you want for little or nothing down, but it doesn't take long for those "small, easy-to-pay monthly installments" to get completely out of hand. They may seem reasonable individually, but when three or four are combined you've bought trouble. When you add the cost of food, shelter, and clothing to a couple of casually acquired monthly payments, you can get into trouble in a hurry. Then you're faced with some really unpleasant, almost impossible choices on the way to go and things you must do without.

That's why you and your wife together must be clear on how much money you have available and on the best way to dispense it. If you haven't already considered it jointly you'd better do so right now. You simply cannot afford to wait any longer because of the real economic dangers you face. Either or both of you may not want to take this step, may even be avoiding it because you don't want to face up to what you suspect you're going to find. But you really have no choice.

Your success or failures in this inquiry depends on how badly you want it to work and the kind of discipline you and your wife are able to bring to it. However, there are a few simple guidelines that can help you in your quest. First, you must be realistic about your situation and confine your concern to your own problems. Don't worry about what other people are doing, or seem to be doing, because their circumstances do not apply to you.

Second, after you have decided exactly where you are financially, you should create a budget based on what you have to work with. Don't bet on what your income *could* be, because that promised raise or bonus is not yours until it is firmly in hand. It's imperative that you budget on real, guaranteed income.

Start with the basics, the rock-bottom essentials. Again, be realistic about how much you need; you're only hurting yourself if you don't. Then decide what to do with what's left. And don't deceive yourselves on what's really necessary—there are many nice things you don't want to do without, but which are not really basics. If you keep them, and you probably will, you should still be straight on where they fit into the scheme of things so that in the event of a crunch you'll know they're optional.

Then together see what you'd like to do with the money left over. The importance of doing it together cannot be overemphasized. This may give rise to tense moments and tight lips, but these should be temporary and are well worth the

eventual result. In establishing priorities, follow the line of
what you've already decided is important to you. With that
step out of the way, deciding where to spend your money is
much easier. And in deciding, look for ways to economize.
There are many things that are marginal when examined more
closely. Don't let peer pressure unduly influence you.

It's important that you don't plan to spend everything that
comes in. Start a regular savings plan, no matter how small.
This is an investment you cannot afford to go without, no matter how much it hurts or how impossible it seems. Put at least
something away that you never touch and just let it grow. It's
surprising how just a little regular sum can add up, and in the
long run it will be worth more than what you're now spending
every cent on. Besides you never know when something unexpected or catastrophic is going to happen and you will really
need to have some reserve cash laid by. With children you
have to consider college, weddings, and who knows what else.
These are things you must anticipate and prepare for, and the
time to start is now.

Unless, of course, you're already so deep in debt that your
outgo is appreciably more than your income and you're sink-
ing further into the red every day. If that's the case, don't keep
kidding yourself about your situation, about the ship that's
going to come in some day. It's nice to dream, but we're living
in a real world where creditors repossess and file lawsuits and
generally act nasty when they're not paid. It may be a bitter
pill but you've got to face facts and make your wife face them
too. It's better to do it now, no matter how much it hurts, than
to get so far behind that you can never work out of it.

If you need professional advice, get it—it's no crime, and
your temporary embarrassment is well worth what you can get
out of it. And stay away from loan sharks. Easy money always
has strings and exhorbitant interest can be an unsuspected
killer. Talk to your banker or some other reliable source,
someone trustworthy who you can be honest with and who
will be honest with you. The first step is to take that hard look
at your situation and, if you've reached the danger zone, do
whatever you must to get out of it now.

Yes, money is important to a successful marriage, as are

many other factors. The particular problem with money is that it can overshadow the others because it bears on everything to some extent. Even very intelligent couples can get so caught up in a blind pursuit of the dollar that they lose all perspective on everyday values. You may well choose riches as the absolute goal, but you must also realize the price you have to pay. Life is so fleeting it can pass you by or use you up before you even know you've started the run. Don't let it happen to you.

3

Vagaries of company life— paying the piper

THE COMPANY GIVETH and—if you don't perform as you should—the company taketh away. That's because the company is what's paying the bills; it's what buys your groceries and makes it possible for you to have all those nice material things. But a company does all of this only if you in turn are willing and able to do what it asks of you.

This should be pretty obvious, and few people expect to keep a job when their performance is below company expectations. Of course, there are many who have one perspective of how they're doing while the company has another, but that is something else again. The only way a company can make the money to pay the people working for it is by having those employed do their assigned work. And that, basically, is what a company is: people working together so the company can make money so all of the people working for it can make money. You go to work, do the job, and get paid for it. What could be simpler?

But it's never as simple in practice as it sounds, and that's where the problem lies. It can be hard for your wife to see that virtually everything the company asks you to do is proper.

Many times she feels you're being asked to do far more than the company has a right to ask. Sometimes she's correct, but often she's way off base, and it's hard to make her see that. When you try to explain why, she has difficulty getting a handle on the hidden responsibilities. It's especially hard if she sees the job as a rival for your attention.

You may feel that this is ridiculous, but from her point of view she is sure she's getting a bad deal. Her emotions enter into her thinking, and reasoning goes by the wayside. All she knows is that you seem to be giving more to the company than to her, and she can't understand why. She knows you're doing a good job; she knows you work hard; she knows you're giving the firm a darn good return for the money it's paying you. So why give it more of your valuable time than is absolutely necessary? Why not reserve that time for her?

That's a good question. Why not indeed? The answer seems clear in your mind, but you come up short in explaining. You try to point out how your job is more than any dry, detailed job description can indicate. It's people and duty and obligations and pride and accomplishing. The fact is, if you're in the right job, there'll be a part of you that will always be beyond explaining, even to someone as close as your wife.

But hard as it is, you must try to explain why there are certain things you have to do even though they might be outside a strict interpretation of a job. How your wife views your work has a direct bearing on how well you are able to do that job. To do it right you need her support, and for her to give it she must understand what your job means to you.

You will probably need to make her understand that the people you work with are significant to you. They fit into your life's total picture, and in a certain sense they are a factor in your marriage. There's no way to separate them from your life at home, and that's something you should try to make your wife understand.

You influence the lives of those who work with you and they in turn influence yours. They are of your world and as such demand a bit of you, a portion that your wife might rightfully claim as hers. They tug on invisible strings that have a very real connection. This can create a definite bind for her and it's up to you to make her aware of these influences on your marriage. Remember that you are moving in a world that is foreign to her, but that vitally affects her anyway.

Think about it for a minute: you probably know a lot more about her world and the people in it than she does about yours. Therefore, make her aware, fill her in, let her take part in your other life as much as possible. Let her share, enjoy, empathize, and feel the same enthusiasm about the job you feel. Job and wife are both so much a part of you that the only way you can get the most from each is by bringing them together, minimizing the different pulls as much as possible.

You must do your best to make her aware of what company life is all about, and you must do your best to include her and at the same time protect her. Essential to this is her grasp of the various influences on you at the office and how they affect you. You must enlighten her as to how she must act and react to the people there, and she needs to understand what burdens may be placed on her by the fact that she is married to you.

Remember, however, it's only through you that she can know what's acceptable, legitimate behavior and what's not. Brief her on the lines she doesn't have to cross, the things that will come her way but that she doesn't have to handle. She will know only if you help her to know the mysteries, the expectations, the pushes and pulls of your other life.

The Boss

Whether young or old, male or female, a socializer or a workaholic, pleasant or unpleasant, the boss has a special sort of influence on your marriage. Good or bad, it's an association you have no choice but to live with. Your boss is the one individual who can throw a monkey wrench into a carefully planned family project at the last minute. He is also the one who can give you that little extra break just when you or your wife needs it.

The person you report to can make your married life miserable just by the treatment given you during the day. If you don't like your boss or the way he deals with you, it can affect your whole attitude at home. If he is unreasonable in his demands on your time, it will definitely affect your moods and those of your wife. The situation is worse when the boss has no regard for family life, yours or his. It can get tricky if the boss is overly fond of you. Or of your wife. Or if the boss's own marriage is warped or guided by standards different from yours.

It's highly improbable that you, your boss, and your wife will never be together. When you are, fireworks can explode or honey can flow. However you steer it, remember one thing: he's your boss, not hers.

In this day and age, even wives who stay at home can be vehement about their prerogatives as free people. There are those—not necessarily in the minority—who not only see no reason to kowtow to hubby's boss, but take an almost perverse delight in going to the other extreme. They are bent on proving their independence by an irreverence which at times may border on insolence. If you've got a wife like this, even if she sees your boss just once in a while, you're going to have some very tense moments.

Your wife's opinion of the boss is very important. If she doesn't like him you're not going to get much sympathy when you have to change plans at the last minute because of him. And you're not going to get much support when required to go above and beyond, because it's the request of someone your wife doesn't like.

There's also the opposite danger: the boss could strike a positive chord in your spouse, not romantic in most cases, but one that makes her want to side with him instead of with you. Since she's not with him every day as you are there's no way she can understand what a louse he can be. All she sees is the nice guy bit, and when you really need her sympathy because he has abused you or taken advantage of you, she can't understand and withholds her support.

One way or another the boss is going to be an influence. Even in the unlikely event there is no contact whatever, the way you're treated on the job has a great effect on your off-the-job frame of mind. This is going to be a factor in your marriage unless you work to counter the effects.

Your first challenge is to leave the boss at the office. That's

easier said than done, of course, but when at home don't let
your boss dominate your thoughts. Give him his due on the job
even if you don't like him. If he's a bother, be bothered at the
office. But don't let it also bother your wife. The same is true if
he's wonderful: enjoy him *at work*. Certainly if there's a real
problem to be discussed, you should. But as far as the everyday petty hassles go, leave them at your door.

While we're at it, don't let the boss dominate you. It's easy
to let that happen if he's the strong and demanding type, but
you must fight to remain your own person. Though you are
subject to all kinds of pressure, draw the line in your own mind
about your boss's requirements and what is owed to your
family. In fact, how dominant the boss is depends to a large
extent on what you allow or don't allow.

You and your spouse should have an understanding about
your boss. What do you expect of her? How should she act in
his presence? Even though she is not an employee, there is a
sort of behavior that is proper for her when with him. Does she
understand this? Can a social misunderstanding or slight carry
over onto the job? Can your spouse really make an important
difference in your future? Of course she can. And she should
know that by virtue of being your wife she has a responsibility
to support you and not undermine your relationship with your
superiors or peers. She should know that she can be a definite
factor in your career.

But she should also know you do not expect her to be an
indentured servant; that along with the obligation to support
she has many freedoms. There is no reason, for example, for
her to take abuse or insults or passes or anything else out of
line. And if you expect her to, you'd better reevaluate your
marriage and your role in the company.

Mrs. Boss

Now a word about Mrs. Boss. Strictly speaking she
shouldn't be a concern, because she has no official connection
with you or your wife. But in reality, she is a factor.

Down through the ages all bosses have been heavily influenced by their wives, and the modern boss is no exception. By his very proximity and continual exposure to her, her opinions and comments have to carry some weight. If she should so choose, she can easily level a few well-chosen words on any subject—including you—whether it's her place to or not. And there's scarcely a man alive who can ignore an idea completely once it's been put in his mind.

For that reason you can never be sure what sort of influence your boss's wife has. Is it great or nonexistent? Will it affect you or not? Is the strong man at the office a puppy dog at home? Does she like or dislike you? You might say it doesn't matter to you one way or the other. You work for the company just like your boss, and his wife's opinion doesn't have to do with you. You can stick out your chin and say that that's the way it should be and that's the way it will be. Period.

That's fine, only take it easy. Keep some of these thoughts to yourself. After all, she is still the boss's wife and should be afforded a certain amount of respect. It doesn't make you a toady if you acknowledge her place and give her the proper respect. You don't have to like her to be courteous, and it's not politicking if you pay her the proper respect. And if she's a pain to the boss, that's for him to decide. He'll surely resent one of his juniors being openly critical of his wife.

If she does try to intrude on your life, try to turn her aside diplomatically. There's no sense antagonizing her if you don't have to. But you're absolutely right about one thing: you don't work for her, and there's no reason to act as if you do. This may take some occasional fancy footwork but it can be done. If it does get unbearable, you've got to figure some way around it. It's possible that a face-to-face confrontation with her will do the trick, especially if you approach her civilly. But of course it could also backfire. If you're afraid to take that risk, it may be more appropriate to go directly to your boss. This isn't a bad approach if you are prepared, if you limit yourself to specific points, and have a positive attitude about it. Present it as a problem. Don't go to him with a chip on your shoulder ready to call names. Be honest, not petty.

There is some risk to your job in deciding whether to approach him or his wife, but it's one you'll have to take if you have this problem. You cannot allow yourself or your wife to be ruled by the boss's wife. When that starts to happen you must stop it any way you can.

The line of what's acceptable should be fairly clear to you. There is a certain amount of catering that is propitious whether it goes against your grain or not. At least you can live with it. But there is also a line you can't—or shouldn't—cross, because once you do you start working for your boss's wife as well as her husband. There may be areas where you're not really sure if it's courtesy or obedience, but if a pattern begins to emerge, do what you must to get back on the proper side of the line. And once there, stay on the right side of it.

This line is not nearly so clear for your wife, though you might think there shouldn't be any question at all. Neither woman works for the company and there's no official relationship between them. On the surface there's no reason your wife should be subject to the commands and whims of the boss's wife.

However, this is another one of those gray areas. There is a very real relationship between them by virtue of yours with your boss. There's no getting around it: the problem can get sticky for your spouse if the other woman tries to make their relationship more than it is.

For example, say the boss's wife calls and asks your wife to help with a company-related function. What's she supposed to do? She refused to be forced into compliance, and rightfully so, but she also wants to do the right thing. She doesn't mind helping this one time, but she knows what will happen later, having seen it happen to others. She also thinks you're sharp enough to make it on your own and doesn't want to put an unnecessary hurdle in your path.

There are some important considerations to work out here. Does your position require allegiance and a subservient role for wife? How much of her own life should she sacrifice? By being drawn into your boss's wife's web, there's the danger your wife will not have time to cultivate and enjoy a life and friends of her own. Just being nice can induce Mrs. Boss to act as though your wife is supposed to do her bidding.

There is no hard and fast rule, so the necessary thing for

you and your wife to do is figure out what's important to you both. Even if you don't see eye to eye straight down the line, there should be agreement on the boundaries of your relationship. Each of you should know what the other won't and will accept.

There are many different types of bosses and wives and you can never consider or treat them all the same. You and your wife should be flexible, then. There will be some give and take for both of you, and cases where more effort on your part is expected but worth it. In the final analysis you must both agree that the boss's wife is part of the job, whether it's in the job description or not.

Office Politics

Whether your office is large or small, rural or urban, deals in manufacturing or a service, you're going to be subjected to and involved in office politics. Even the nicest people just can't seem to avoid it. You may not want any part of it, but there's no way to escape the effects.

The smartest thing is to rise above politics if you possibly can, but the talk, gossip, and machinations will still go on all around you. Granted, it's all very silly and you shouldn't have to be concerned, but it's there, and the way some people play the game, it's not so funny.

That's how you get involved. If you're a comer, then you are a threat to at least one person and probably several. That's nothing you can help. If you're good you're going to push ahead, and you should. But you are going to cause resentment, fear, and jealousy. You may think of yourself as a nice guy with only a few, not very obvious, faults, but that's not necessarily the way you seem to your co-workers. You are the one who got the promotion; or who forced their lifelong friend out; or the glory hog who gets the credit for their work. There have been volumes written about office politics, and for good reasons. While most offices are congenial they can be vicious when groups are sharply polarized, back stabbers run rampant, and every person in the place is fair game.

In such a setting, you are vulnerable whether you participate or not. You cannot afford to act like an ostrich. Don't get
drawn in. And don't let your wife become inadvertently drawn
in either.

You might think this is another area where your wife
wouldn't be included by any reasonable stretch of the imagi-
nation. After all, why should office in-fighting concern her?
How is she supposed to know that there are some people she
should speak to; some she should ignore; some who are nice to
her yet are cold as death to her husband; that the one she just
raved about to the boss is the very one who tried to pull the rug
out from under you; that the gray-haired secretary who is always so nice and friendly is merely trying to pump her for
information?

The only way she has a chance to know all these things is if
you let her in on what's going on. This is tricky because what
seems so obvious at the office when you're experiencing it can
appear ridiculous when told at home. It can be hard to make
your wife understand just what it is you're telling her and·why.
It's likely she'll poke holes in your scenario because it sounds
so implausible—and in the retelling you might wonder if
you're being paranoid.

Besides all of this, she may not see what it has to do with
her. After all, you're the one with the job, office personalities
are your problem. That's a good argument, but real life doesn't
work that way. The rest of the world won't let it. It can be very
exasperating trying to make your wife see the way it really is.
You have the advantage of actually being in the office and
seeing how people operate. But try to help her also be aware,
because it can and does affect her.

If you're lucky, office politicking is at a minimum where
you work. The intensity varies from place to place, and the
person running things can make a great deal of difference as to
how much—which is a lesson you ought never forget as you
move up the ladder. The amount of flak you get depends on
your position. At the lower end of the spectrum, when you're
beginning, things aren't so bad; but when you start moving, or
if you've been brought in fairly high, watch out. That's when
office politics comes into full play.

Even when people don't intend to be malicious they can wind up that way, because humans are incorrigible meddlers and gossipers. Add to that the fast pace and insecurities of the modern business world and you begin to understand how house politics can bring down the strong. So, keep your wits about you—it's only too easy to get drawn into the behind-the-scenes skullduggeries. And when you get involved the chances of your wife becoming subject to it are that much greater. You have an obligation to keep the unpleasant realities of your office from dragging your innocent wife where she doesn't want to go.

Social Politics

Of course, office politics do not stop at the company door. They quite often move to a slightly different sphere, one where you probably need all the help you can get, but one where the sweet, lovely, charming mate at your side feels fairly comfortable. No matter how soft and fragile you may think she is, when she's confronted firsthand with the subtle slights and digs of other women, your wife not only recognizes them, she's probably a whole lot better equipped to deal with them than you are.

Whether it's in her disposition or not to play these games, you can bet your boots she knows when others are playing them. It's common for a man to be a victim of office politics and never know it because he is so immersed in his work. But most women seem to have an instinctive feel for nuances the poor male doesn't even suspect. And while your spouse may not like it, thinks it's silly, and disdains participation, she darn well understands what's happening.

In company social politics you're best advised to let your wife help you. In the first place it gets her more involved in your company life and more a part of your career. And second, being more adept at it, she can steer you through situations you'd surely bungle, left to your own devices.

Your wife knows when your arch rival is sneaking some points and when someone else is maneuvering, threatening your unprotected flank. This may surprise you if you've never thought of her in that light or if you've never really listened to her. That's perfectly understandable—when you let her in you also admit your own limitations and it can hurt. Sometimes it's hard to know which is worse—the fact that she's right or the fact that she's *aware* that you're not 100 percent perfect. Well, don't let the latter bother you. Whether she ever says it or not, she realized very early in the game that though you may possess a number of good qualities, perfection is not one of them.

Since you do not have to worry about maintaining an image with your wife, you're free to enlist her aid and support in your company-related social battles. She can be a tremendous ally if you include her in the action, letting her know she has a prime role and that you have confidence in and are counting on her. Let her arrange the dinners, parties, and teas; let her suggest whom to invite home and when; let her help decide whom to entertain out; and who is worth doing what for.

It's very rare that a man's social activities will get him a promotion, although it sometimes seems that way. What does happen is that between two equal candidates, the one whose social graces—and politics—conform more closely to the boss's will get the nod. It's no secret that many companies are now looking to advance the "whole man," the whole man being one whose wife steers, guides, and complements him in the execution of the social graces. Even if you are not playing the corporate promotion game, there are social responsibilities in your job and your wife knows what's best.

So put the talents of your wife to good use. She's almost bound to have knowledge you need. Don't hurt yourself unnecessarily by excluding her. Don't be an otherwise brilliant performer who fails to perceive what the female instinctively knows.

An Unhappy Wife

It's important to include your wife wherever and whenever possible. It's important that she feels part of your work world, that she knows you consider her a vital and valuable part of your on-the-job life. If she doesn't or isn't allowed to feel this way you run the danger of either losing her or living through some very trying, taxing, unhappy times with her.

One of the failings of the modern business world is that it leaves wives out of things, giving them no role or sense of participation. It can be rough for a woman who wants to give her all to her husband and who strongly believes that her place is at his side only to find it's not that way at all.

The company signs her husband, maybe even after a husband-and-wife team talk, but once he's in the fold there's no place for her. The woman could have two heads and it wouldn't matter as long as she stays in her place and the husband does his job. For any woman wanting to be a helpmate, this is hard to take and can lead to frustrations, disappointments, and eventually to considerable unhappiness. That's why it is critical to make her a part of what you're doing. Otherwise, she may develop powerful feelings of isolation and alienation because neither you nor the company needs anything from her. You can mitigate this to a considerable extent by making her see that she is a part of what you're doing and that you need her support.

Help her to understand that she does have a purpose, especially if she has a hard time seeing it. This is more than just an exercise in doing the nice husbandly thing. If your wife is unhappy at home it is going to have an adverse effect on what you do at work. The unhappier she is, the more it's going to distract you on the job.

Remember this: if your wife doesn't feel useful from the start, she never will. As you develop she will be left behind, uncertain as to where you're going and what her place in that drive could ever be. Then she'll either figuratively or literally drop by the wayside. You may rationalize that, well, she can find something to pursue on her own, but to the extent that it is completely separate and distinct from you, you'll eventually feel the loss. That's the lesson of the unhappy spouse; if you let it happen you're going to someday suffer personally and probably professionally.

Take a hard look right now at the circumstances of your wife. Is she happy or unhappy? Was she completely honest when you reviewed what was important to both of you? Have you let her fight the battle of unhappiness by herself, not caring, not sharing, not including, not supporting? If so, look at what it's done to her and be objective in your evaluation. Can you see where you've not given what she needed, or where she had to fight some pretty rough battles on her own? Have you let her become—even contributed to her becoming—an unhappy wife?

If that's the case, you must correct this very bad situation. Look for the root of the problem. Have you simply been more attached to the company than to her? Have you kept her from the problems of office politics and denied her a major role in the social battles? Does she understand your boss and his place in your marriage? Have you betrayed her in her dealings with Mrs. Boss? Most importantly, have you made her feel that she doesn't count in your own success?

If you answered yes to any of the above questions, now is the time to start correcting your mistake. It won't be an overnight chore if she's truly unhappy. You'd better face it. Whereas the company has been an unwitting accomplice, you have been an only-too-willing culprit and an unpardonable one if you don't do your utmost to set things right. You must realize that the rigors of your job, good job that it is, can make your wife a company widow.

Look closely to see whether she is happy and think carefully what you can and must do to make or keep her so. And don't expect any miracles just because you've seen the light. It may take a while but if you are concerned enough to try to make her happy again you can. It's like everything else in marriage; if you abandon your wife and don't let her help you, the marriage will eventually be lost and then you'll be the loser, as hurt and unhappy as she.

An Uncooperative Wife

If your wife is unhappy for reasons related to your company and its shortcomings, you can do certain things to counteract it. But it's another story if she is uncooperative rather than unhappy. She may get to be this way for reasons that make sense only to her, but then that's what is important.

Maybe she is of the "new generation" that doesn't believe in all of this "corporate crap." You can play that game if you want, she'll say, but she's not going to. Maybe she started off unhappy and worked herself out of it but in so doing became disenchanted, alienated, and anti-company. She was hurt by the firm so why give it anything in return? Or maybe she just can't see any point to all that Mickey Mouse stuff. Whatever the reason, if your wife is uncooperative you've got a problem that will get worse unless you do something about it. Maybe you can maintain your dedication to your job in the face of your wife's antagonism, and maybe not. But since failure is a very real possibility, you had better take some corrective action. Go back to the basics of what's important to you and to her. Was there really an accord or were you both just going through the motions?

One way or another things will have to change. Whether your wife believes in your job or not, the fact that it is important to you should be enough in and of itself for her to cooperate. Even if she feels fractious, rebellious and unhappy, the very fact that you feel she should cooperate should be sufficient reason for her. An uncooperative wife may not hinder you to the point of your becoming ineffective, but she will hurt your performance. It's just so much easier on the job when you have the understanding and support from your wife.

If you've reached this kind of impasse you must do everything you can to get out of it, even going so far as questioning whether the company life is for you if it's so alien to your wife. Some deep soul searching is called for to find the root of the problem. You have to face the reasons for her uncooperativeness, and consider the consequences of it, including the possibility of ruin to you, your job, and your marriage.

Evaluating Worth

And as you look for reasons why your wife is unhappy or uncooperative, take a good look at the company and yourself.

What kind of company is it? Is it one you have confidence in and that treats you and everybody else as it should? Is it fair in dealing with new employees and older employees? Is it the kind of place you would want your kids to spend their lives in? Does it make unjust demands on you without reciprocating the loyalty it expects from you? Do you resent the extra time you must give, even though you feel duty bound to give it? Is it the kind of company you envisioned when you searched your soul to really know what you want out of life?

Then there's the boss. How do you get along with him? How would you evaluate him? Satisfaction doesn't have to be only a one-way street, and you should be doing some judging of your own. Is your boss the kind who makes your days so miserable that you grow horns when you go home at night? Is he the kind who schedules work for you without consideration or notice? Does he have any respect for your home life and responsibilities to your wife? How about his wife? Does she intrude on you and yours? Is she a person you should answer to? And what about office politics? Do you know what's going on? Have you helped your wife understand what happens there and does she lend help and support? Do you seek her help in brunting the effect of office politics that carry over into your social life? Do the politics in general intrude too much in your life?

Then you must look at how happy your wife is. Including her in your office life, seeking her help with job-related problems will boost her spirits considerably. If she's not happy, try to figure out why. Is it temporary, a natural change of mood due to problems having nothing to do with you per se? Or is it continual? Find out and do something positive about it.

This also applies if she's being uncooperative. It may not be the kiss of death, but it can add considerably to the normal conflicts between job and marriage. It's even possible it will place an intolerable burden on one of you, so get to the bottom of the problem as quickly as possible.

What it finally will come to in the end is questioning whether this company, or any company, is right for you and your marriage. If you work in an atmosphere where wives are routinely ignored, can you stay? Do you share that antique attitude or do you feel the company should regard her as an important extension of your whole self and treat her accordingly?

Your wife is important to your career even when she is following a career of her own. You, your job, and your wife are all so intertwined you can never have a neat separation. Don't try. Company life can be good for you and your marriage if you first set the standards and then find a company that supports your notions. You're going to have to pay the piper somewhere, somehow, so do it with the knowledge that whatever else happens it's better to do it with a wife who is as important to you as you are to her.

4

Keep the line open

ONE OF THE MOST WIDELY used words today is communication. Business leaders say that most of their problems would be solved if they had better communication; educators say one of the greatest weaknesses in the educational system is that it doesn't teach students how to communicate; and a whole new industry has come into being because of the expanding information business and people's need to know. It's important in business; it's important in living, and it's critically important in marriage.

Of all the many tragedies that can happen in a marriage, there's none greater or more damaging than lack of proper communication between husband and wife. It can be both a casualty and the cause of a poor marriage, for if it's not there the marriage will never be what it could be.

Communication in marriage is not just speaking to one another politely, exchanging routine pleasantries, or passing basic information. It's a way of living together totally, with a complete sharing of thoughts, ideas, emotions, feelings, dreams, wants and all of what makes two people a couple. It's the mutual give and take that comes from intimately knowing what each needs and expects and even demands from the other. True communication between partners serves to make a strong bond stronger and will help keep a marriage from deteriorating.

So don't cheat yourself and your marriage by not taking advantage of this wonderful, simple, life-sustaining tool that is available to each and every married couple. Look at your marriage in terms of the kind of communication you and your wife have. How does it stack up with what it should be? Do you really communicate with one another or are you just going through the motions? When your wife talks to you, do you resort to automatic responses to pacify her? Are you frustrated when you talk to her because it seems that she never pays attention to anything you say? Are you frequently embarrassed when you're supposed to have done something, and you don't even remember agreeing to do it because you didn't pay attention when your wife was talking about it?

If these kinds of things are happening to you, chances are you have a serious communication problem in your home, which tells you that you're losing a lot from your marriage. You are in effect two people living separate lives although sharing a common home and perhaps a few common interests. If you let this happen, you and your wife are cheating yourselves out of the best part—trust and real understanding. Start looking right away to see if you are guilty and, if so, start searching for ways to overcome it.

As with most of the troubles in marriage, the best place to look for the cause is with yourself. It's not a question of intent, or being good or bad, or even knowing you're doing wrong. Like so many weaknesses, there can be an unnoticed erosion of the precious ability to really talk which means to really share.

The first step, then, is to understand that there *is* a potential danger, that something is missing. Begin your analysis by looking at the simple act of conversing. Do you speak to your wife as though she's a real person? Or do you talk at her as if she's a child or a moron? Maybe you talk around your wife as if she's not really there? Or, and you have to be truthful with yourself here, do you even bother to talk to your wife at all? Assuming you do, do you talk to her really believing she's important enough to hear what you have to say, that she's worth sharing your thinking with?

Conversely, do you really listen to what she says to you? Is what she says worth putting the newspaper aside for so you can give her some attention? Or do you let television take the place of the normal and healthy conversation that should be a part of your life? There's no way to maintain a running conversation all the time, but there has to be a dialog that is genuine.

When there is, when you really start communicating as you should, when you actually listen and she can count on you to listen, any prattle that you have had to contend with will diminish, too. When your wife knows she will have your ear when she needs it she won't have to drown you in chatter. And she will also know she won't have to keep harping at you to tell her what's going on. When she can count on a mutual give and take, the two of you can communicate in a much more relaxed and pleasing manner.

In fact, true communication can open up a whole new way of life. You can recapture the rapport you once had rather than let it go with the passage of time or the development of bad habits. The act of talking is a natural impulse, so take advantage of it to make your life a little better and your marriage considerably stronger.

But, good medicine that talking is, you can't expect any overnight miracles to last if you let the conversation die out. If talking has been a long-term problem with you and your spouse, and now all of a sudden you announce a plan to begin "communicating," she'll probably have a wait-and-see attitude. And even though you may be trying your hardest, it's going to take a little time to develop the talking habit. Old ways are hard to break, and if the attempt doesn't produce immediate results, or is met with skepticism, you're going to ask yourself more than once if it's really worth it. But since you know it is in the long run, it's up to you to get the conversation flowing. When you come home in the evening and your wife is bubbling over about what happened during the day, take the time to listen. Give her a chance to get the tensions and problems off her chest and don't make the mistake of closing her

out because you have no patience or you feel it is of no consequence.

If you continue to listen, it will get through to her that you
do care what she has to say, that she will be heard, and that her
day is important to you. Then gradually she will feel that she
doesn't have to pounce on you to get your attention or be
compelled to pour out her burdens on you without giving you
a chance to spill out yours.

By the same token, you should guard against falling into a
routine of griping the minute you come through the door. Her
initial sympathy can soon wane if all she hears every night is
your continuing monologue of what to her are petty annoyances. Carrying around these minor complaints is probably
not doing you any good, either, so let your developing courtesy for her serve as a mirror for your own conduct. Then when
you do sit down and talk there's not an automatic turn-off on
the part of either of you.

Just keep in mind that one or the other of you may need to
unwind when you first come together. Then, once the petty
items are out of the way, you can focus on mutually rewarding
topics. The petty things will always exist, because you each
confront so much trivia during the course of a normal day, but
you can work it in smoothly and keep it in proper perspective.
Instead of letting it come between you, you might even be
able to laugh at what seemed earth-shattering moments before.

Truth—No Faking

An essential part of communicating in a marriage is complete honesty between partners. The first cardinal rule of your
own survival is total honesty with yourself. The same holds in
dealing with your spouse. You can't make a practice of lying to
her—if you do, you won't have her as your spouse for very long
because she'll inevitably discover the deceit.

Although you may not believe it, she often knows when
you're living a lie even before you know it yourself. She knows
exactly how honest you're being with yourself and with her.

And if you can't be honest with your wife, there's no bedrock for your marriage, and you may as well give it up. Being honest is more than just telling the truth. There has to be an honesty deep inside, including your attitudes and emotions, ideas and thoughts. The only way you can have true harmony and understanding is if there is open and complete honesty between you two. Here again you must measure yourself first.

Are you completely honest with your wife? Do you feel you can lay everything out on the table, or must you hold some things back? Do you do this to protect your wife, or because you think she wouldn't understand, that she would belittle you, or that she may make you finally face reality? But that's what marriage should be—two people facing and conquering problems that, encountered alone, are difficult to endure. What happens when you keep something from your wife is that you take away strength from yourself. You don't fool her, but in shutting her out, you do make her feel rejected, whether you mean to or not. Then a little more substance has gone out of your marriage, and even more when she in turn is constrained in her honesty with you. These little cracks add up, and with time the wholeness that once was or could have been drifts further out of reach. The final casualty is not honesty but the marriage.

Rather than let that happen, think for a minute now what a great loss it would be. Imagine the luxury in this hectic, mercurial, transient world of having someone whom you can be totally, absolutely, completely honest with. Somebody you can relax with because you're not worried about arming yourself with the countless defense mechanisms that have become such a large part of our daily interaction with others; the pure joy of being with someone you can be yourself with, not putting on airs or worrying about her finding your feet made of clay; somebody who cares for you, about you, just as you are, because you are you.

That somebody is right there with you now if you are smart enough to let her be. That's what your wife can and should be to you. That's what your wife will be if you're willing to do what's necessary to have that kind of marriage. You have to be prepared for total honesty on your own part, not the kind where you tell her you hate a new hat she's raving about, but the kind that tells her you want her to see and share all that you are.

With this total honesty you can bring the marriage closer—but note a word of caution. If honesty has not been in the marriage to at least some degree, you can't bring it in overnight. You may well have taken a giant step toward it when discussing what is important to you both, but that one step is just a start. It can, however, serve as a solid foundation to build a new dimension between the two of you.

All in all, you'll be stronger because your wife will help you to see yourself more clearly. You can take her criticism in a spirit that will benefit rather than deflate you. You won't have to pretend to be a superman, and you can accept compliments as sincere, knowing that she doesn't have to flatter you. Of course, with honesty will come some barbs, but the good will far outweigh the bad.

Getting Acquainted

Another great thing that honesty and complete truthfulness will do is help you both get better acquainted. Now you may well say, "What kind of fool notion is that? We have lived together for years, so we certainly should know each other by now." Yes, you should! You should be thoroughly acquainted and know each other like the proverbial book. But what happens too often is that you get used to living with your wife on a surface level. There are so many purely routine aspects of marriage that you stop thinking about what is going on inside, in the heart, mind, and soul of your life's mate. You forget how much depth your wife has and lose track of the warm, wonderful, happy person who attracted you in the first place. A plateau of coexistence is reached and your wife becomes a one-dimensional by-product of the marriage, a large part of her neglected and forgotten.

Before you shrug your shoulders and say that this is non-sense and doesn't apply to you, do a little soul searching and reflecting. If you are honest, and if your memory serves you well, there was an incident in the not-too-distant past when your wife really surprised you. Perhaps she brought up a subject you didn't know she was interested in; displayed a solid grasp of something you didn't know she knew about; expressed a strong feeling about something you had no idea she cared about; or did something that came as a complete surprise because it was so much out of character.

If you search your memory a little further, you'll remember other comments that caught you off guard because they were so unexpected coming from her. But surprised you shouldn't have been because those unexpected, infrequent comments or actions offered a flash of the person you're living with. A person you may have forgotten dwells within that familiar entity you call wife.

It's sad, but what happens in too many marriages is that the partners get so caught up in the routine that they reach a limit in their knowledge of each other and literally stop being acquainted. When you consider that it takes years and years to get to know yourself at all, it should give you an idea of how difficult it is to get to know someone else, even someone you live with day in and day out. And it's hard to want to know that person if you fail to see her as a living, growing, changing, inviting, enticing human being.

There's another part of getting acquainted. There's no way you can really know each other before marriage—even if you lived together it's not the same—hence, much of the getting to know one another happens afterwards. Combine that with the fact that neither of you is now the same person you were when first married, and you can see the challenge and need of getting and staying acquainted.

If you don't you'll miss a very special part of living together. One of the real delights in married life is discovering who that person you married really is, especially in the sense of what kind of entity the two of you make, being one as a couple yet remaining two separate, distinct persons. It's seeing and feeling and enjoying her as an extension of your own self and letting her add a new dimension to your character.

When you really get to know her, you gain a better appreciation of this wonderful creature who also happens to be your wife. You discover that there is much more there than you realized. If it's been awhile since you've thought about it, rediscover those qualities that first brought you together and those that made you want to stay together. Can you still remember them? They're there somewhere if you're up to bringing them out again.

It's quite a challenge if you've ignored them and let them die and virtually impossible if you've let the qualities in you that attracted her die also. But is this really the case with you? Answer truthfully if you want to bring the bloom back to her cheeks and your marriage. It may take a lot of effort to bring those qualities back. They may have been buried or denied so long that she too has forgotten she once had them. Familiarity may have blinded you to the person you once knew, but there's probably a lot more depth there than you can appreciate at first glance.

Of course you may be wondering why, if these qualities are still there, aren't they more apparent? But the same thing has probably happened to you to a greater or lesser extent, so look at yourself for the answer. Mentally bring your wife's and your hidden or suppressed or dying true selves out into the open. See her again as a complete, multidimensional person in her own right. Then, sticking with the basics, start talking with her again. Show her that you still have some of the same qualities she first saw in you. Let her get reacquainted with you as you are now. After all, just as you can remember her surprising you, no doubt you have done the same to her (only probably not as much).

The classic line may be, "My wife doesn't understand me," but the truth usually is that she understands you all too well. Even so, just as you've lost track of your wife, some of you has slipped away from her, too. Make the move to get really acquainted. You'll find unsuspected delights that will brighten your taken-for-granted, used-to-each-other, one-dimensional-life-together that has been disguised as a marriage, and make it real.

Your Best Friend

Having begun to re-experience each other, you're well on your way to having an invaluable asset as you fight your way upward in the corporate world—a friend.

It's often said that it's impossible to have a true friend at work because you will eventually end up competing, that sooner or later if you both are sharp enough you will come to be at odds. This may seem pretty cynical—and maybe it is—but it is also somewhat true. Not because everybody is madly plotting against everybody else, or because your associates are all trying to cut your throat, but because each person has his own particular interests, which are never exactly compatible with anyone else's. Where there have been mutually beneficial, dual corporate climbs it's been because they both accommodated one leader. When that doesn't exist in some form, it's hard to find anyone you can ever truly, for all times' sake, count as your friend—except for one: your wife.

Then, who is more available to do things with? Who else can almost always get out the same night you can? Who else is easier to travel with wherever you are going? And who else can really understand your deep questions about life itself, it's problems and rewards? And who else is so completely concerned with your destiny and what it means to you? Who else is sharing that destiny?

The fact is there's no one as involved or potentially interested in you as your wife. Therefore no one else is in a position to be the kind of personal friend she can be. But it's up to you to convert her potential as a friend to the reality of being one. That's the true goal of communication in marriage. You've gone to the heart of married communication when you and your wife have developed into something much more than lovers consuming each other's lives. If you do not consider your wife a friend, you're missing one of the greatest gifts of married life. No matter how good you may think your marriage is right now, unless you and your wife are friends, really liking each other as people, you're going to go through life shortchanging yourselves.

Everyone should have at least one close friend. Those who have more than one are rich beyond measure. Boyhood and school chums are great, but the years apart make a difference. There are changes in people themselves, the way they relate to life and the pattern of experiences they have had. Be honest—how much in common did you have the last time you saw your best boyhood friend? How long before you ran out of things to say and began to get uncomfortable?

It's the same with people you meet in the corporate world. They come and go and are to be enjoyed for the moment, but there are limits. That doesn't mean you should not pursue a friendship, or that you should think the only friendship that has any meaning is the one with your wife. Quite the contrary. If your relationship with your wife is as it should be, then your other friendships can be that much better. Your wife will not see them as competition, and she will be secure enough to encourage them. You'll be able to include and exclude her whenever it's appropriate and you'll be that much richer for it.

Consider how much stronger your wife will be if she can count on you as a sustaining friend. She'll still need others, and you should encourage her to have others. Unfortunately, some of the constraints of company living do not always leave her much latitude for developing the kind of friends she wants or should have. Besides, deep friendships take time, especially as you get a little older. The main thing is that if you fill the critical need of being her friend, she can be a lot more secure in her dealings with others because she doesn't have to take whatever comes along.

An added benefit is that you and she can have fun together. All this heavy, serious stuff is necessary to think about—there's no way around it in married life—but that's not all there is to it. Who wants to live that way all the time anyway? A great blessing of having a close friend is that you can share the good times, have some laughs, break the everyday tedium together. Your friend your wife is perfect here, so don't deny yourself this treasure. Life is so full of mandatory seriousness that you should break it whenever you can. And the best way to break it is with a friend—the handiest and best friend of all.

The Listener

Another great advantage to having a live-in friend is that it provides something we all crave—and desperately need—a sympathetic listener, a listener who is a real person and not someone who just sits there going through the motions without hearing a word; a listener who is interested, who cares about what is being said, who is as concerned about what you are saying as you are—a listener who really is your friend.

Think of the advantage that such a listener would give you in performing your job. There are so many ideas and thoughts that you could clarify just by talking about them with someone. It's not so much the answers or critiques that help as it is actually vocalizing them, but often there's no opportunity. Therefore, use the one listener with no ax to grind, the one who presents no danger of stealing your ideas, the one who is capable of questioning or venturing criticism without crushing your ego. That's right—your wife, a listener who you know is not trying to shoot you down but will still question occasional aspects of your basic thinking. And don't ever believe your wife can't question you just because she's not your equal on technical matters. With her as listener, you can express half-formed thoughts you wouldn't dare say to competitive contemporaries, letting the ideas flow naturally and openly.

By taking criticism in the spirit it is given, you get a whole new perspective on your own ideas. No one person can think of everything pertaining to new concepts, and everyone can use all the help available. Maybe you don't think your wife has that much to offer, but if you're willing to take it she's got it to give. Just don't let your ego get in the way the first time she so quietly and deftly bursts your bubble; take and use constructively what she has to say, even if you don't like it. But if she never objects to anything, you're still way ahead by having someone you can talk to.

And it's not always ideas and thoughts that you need to get off your chest. Sometimes you need to talk just to keep from exploding. Self-discipline and stoic bearing may be fine qualities, but you can repress some emotions only so long until you must bring them out into the open. And what better person than your wife and friend who is willing to listen and sympathize no matter what's wrong. It works the other way too. You can do a great service to your wife by listening to her when she needs someone to talk to. She's no more immune than you are to everyday pressures that can build and build. But what can make it bearable for her is knowing that she does have someone she can unload on, someone she can pour her frustrations out to, someone who cares enough to listen, someone who will do for her what she does for you—give that sympathetic ear.

It's not always easy to listen and sympathize. It might seem that many of the things she's bothering you with are minor or a repetition of the same thing she's gone over before. She might have a habit of hitting you with all of her mundane problems the second you come home, no matter when that is. Or you might have something of your own to talk about that seems much more important, and you think she should be listening to you rather than the other way around. It might not be handy to listen when she wants to talk, and you have a hard time not showing your irritation.

Then instead of the listener she needs, you become an antagonist, which only adds to her problems. It makes "friendship" a one-sided relationship and makes for a very unhappy spouse. When that happens you're not doing your part as a friend. And since you can't be bothered with listening to her, why should she bother listening to you? If you know how important it is for you to have someone who listens to you, you should know how important it is for her and care enough to do it.

Start by being the listener yourself. At the same time gradually let your wife know you are going to be counting on her too. She may be slow picking up what you are trying to do, in which case you must lead by example using patience and discipline and, at first, over-listening. Eventually she'll do the same for you and you'll both enjoy a great luxury so many couples never attain.

Growing Together

Yet another reason for close communication between you and your wife is that it will allow you to grow and develop together. Just the simple act of talking has a positive influence and if the dialog is totally honest, it will add strength to the marriage. But only when partners want to succeed can a marriage sustain that kind of openness. As you get better acquainted you come to have a greater appreciation of each other, a greater affection and, finally, an abiding friendship. With that friendship you cement the strengthening bond and lay the basis for the two of you to develop together.

This mutual development is something you must have if your marriage is going to thrive. Nothing remains the same in life, including people. Years of working and experiencing and associating with others bring influences that change opinions, thoughts, and desires. Add to this the individual peculiarities of growing older, and it is obvious that each and every person must change.

The same holds true for husband and wife, but evolving does not have to mean adversity in the marriage. In fact, it can and should result in just the opposite. By the continual give and take that should be a part of every marriage the partners can sense and feel the changes in each other. Continual communication not only keeps both aware of what's happening to the other but it also helps to influence the tempo of change and the nature of the changes that occur in both. By being closely attuned to each other they can follow the same path of development.

Drawing Apart

Consider, for a moment, the alternative. If you're changing and she's changing but the changes aren't in the same direction, there's no way around the fact that sooner or later you're going to drift completely apart. It's something you cannot escape if your marriage doesn't have that basic, continuing communication. And if it does happen, it'll be in large part because the life you're living now isn't much of a married life. Something is lacking. Gradually more and more will disappear and then finally all of it. Gone will be the chance for that confidante who can serve you so well. Gone will be the sympathetic listener who allows you to expound and talk and theorize and clarify to your heart's content. Gone would be the opportunity to truly get to know the person with whom you once most wanted to spend your whole lifetime. The loss of this precious individual is not only a possibility but a probability unless you are alert to the signs and reverse the trend.

5

To move or not to move—
and if you do

TO MOVE OR NOT TO MOVE is a question every company man must face. Especially if you are a comer you will be tempted with various offers which will call for a soul-searching evaluation of what is best. These will be offers to move to another company, to another department within the company, or to a new job in a new town with the same or different company. Whenever you get into this situation there are many things that must be considered and the same sort of evaluation techniques should be applied to them all.

First, you must make a realistic appraisal of the new job. New positions often sound much better than they are, and it's easy to leap at the opportunity. But you should know by now that nothing is exactly what it seems. Unfortunately, that is not always learned from experience, thus there's a tendency for people to close their eyes to some very significant realities when they want something.

The first point is to take your time before accepting. Don't let yourself be pushed into making a decision before you have a chance to examine the job closely. Most companies, when they make an offer, want an answer now, they can't afford to wait; they've got to know right away!

And it's usually true to some extent. There is urgency, only it is seldom a case of life and death. But even if it really is critical that a decision be made as soon as possible, it's imperative that you take all the time you need to make a proper decision. You can't sit and think about it forever, nor can you ever be absolutely sure until you roll up your sleeves and get to work, but you do need to resist being unduly pushed. If the company won't give you any time, then you figure that in your decision, too.

What you must remember is that any move you make is critical to your marriage and career. You simply ought not make a major change without deep thought because whether it's staying within a company or switching jobs and city, there are serious ramifications. Don't take it lightly and say blindly that you'll do it if that's what the company wants. Although company loyalty may be a factor, you can get badly burned by making the wrong choice. You have to look before you leap because once you step off the ledge, there's no going back.

Begin your analysis by questioning why there is an opening in the first place. Fight the urge to assume that the opening is a real opportunity until you find out why there is one. This can be very revealing, and even in clouded circumstances it's not that hard to determine. The people in the new location will hold surprisingly little back when questioned directly, even about circumstances that are not supposed to be public knowledge. But it's up to you to ask the right questions. The company is not necessarily hiding anything, but it may not see the need to volunteer everything, either.

It's different if the company that's making the offer *is* trying to hide something. If it is being deliberately evasive or misleading, you're dealing with people you have no business working with. If in response to your questions all you get are platitudes or nothing at all, you had better keep digging. Then if you find anything at all to give you pause, you'd better be mighty careful of what you're getting into. Down the line if it gets to be a case of the company or you, you know who is going to suffer.

There's no good reason for a company to lie about a job being offered. The fact that it's tough or dirty should be no deterrent to the right man. As long as you know what the score is, you shouldn't be frightened away, either. Be that as it may, it's up to you to get all of the appropriate information ahead of time. Analyze the job itself and don't be misled by a title, no matter how good it sounds. Titles vary so much from company to company that jobs can be labeled exactly the same and yet not even be close in work content. Don't fall for a good-sounding title. You might make a checklist of what you need to know about the job in order to evaluate it. But don't try to make the job into something it is not. This is all too common when people want something badly. They delude themselves, deliberately closing their minds to the truth. Guard against this happening to you.

Is It Right for You?

In your evaluation you must also remember that even though it may not be the job you want for all time, this doesn't automatically disqualify it from being good for you now. Very seldom will you find the ideal job. Therefore, pay attention to some of the minor aspects of the job under consideration. This is the kind of scrutiny your wife can help you with. She will both prod you into seeing the good points and keep you from getting carried away with the glitter. Often she will have more insight than you about the real pluses and minuses of the position.

A good wife will ask the questions you don't particularly want to hear and make you pursue full answers when you are satisfied after only half checking. She's good medicine if you don't resent what she has to say. It may be hard on the old male ego to hear your wife speak more truthfully than you, but don't let your pride get in the way of truly benefiting from her wisdom. With your wife's help, be realistic.

And after you get the answers to all the questions on your checklist it's time to draw up another comparative list. List the good features of the job versus the bad. Do it as objectively as possible. Remember, you're laying the groundwork of a decision and, like Sergeant Friday, you want only the facts. Then look at them and see which side outweighs the other. Let your values come into play now, that's what the exercise is designed for, but don't color the facts to make it come out the way you predeterminedly wanted it to. Now do the same with your current job. Be just as objective and honest with yourself. See how each job stacks up in terms of attractive and unattractive features. This will help you to know what you're getting into if you move and whether the positive aspects of your current job outweigh the bad qualities of the new position.

This decision is too important not to have all the facts available, even if it's a hassle assembling them. If you're going to change, change because what is offered is really better. Just getting away from what you have is not enough of a reason in itself, although some people would jump on any pretext at all. Dissatisfaction with part of what they have leads to rejection of the whole. But you cannot afford to grasp at straws.

If you move and it's not what you want, remember, you can't keep jumping for less than justifiable reasons. Job hopping is fine for the right reasons, but to do it in a blind search for fulfillment or whatever will eventually hurt you. We're not talking about making an interim move with a long-range objective in mind. There's nothing wrong with that, especially if you do the company and yourself proud in the interim; it can be a part of your development, and it's not uncommon for the ambitious and productive to staircase their way to the top. But it starts scaring the better companies if it looks as though there is no pattern to your jumping, they feel they won't be able to depend on you for very long.

Job hunting within your company is the same. If there is good reason to pursue something, go to it. But if you're just trying to see what it's like, your performance will probably be poor, and it's only a matter of time before it catches up with you. Once your dissatisfaction with the company becomes apparent, you may be forced to leave.

So don't move, within the company or outside, just for the sake of moving. When you make the move, do so for a good reason, and only after a thorough evaluation and comparison. Be realistic and remember this basic rule: fool the world if you want, but never fool yourself.

Career and Marriage

After you have all the facts, it's time for you to decide in light of the two most important factors in your life, career and marriage. Let's face it, these are what life is all about. They're what all of the why's and wherefore's come down to; throughout your life your decisions will always touch on one or the other. It's the same thing if you move: What will be the effect on your marriage or your career?

Let's take a look at the effects of a move on your career first. If you've done your homework and know what is important to you as a person, your decision-making process will be aided considerably. Knowing where you ultimately want to go is an invaluable aid in deciding what the best path in the short term is. This won't give you all of the answers but will automatically supply some of them. You'll know that no matter how appealing some offers are on the surface they won't be right for you. It works the other way too. Your long-term goals may lead you to accept a job offer that has little initial appeal but makes a lot of sense anyway.

Another reason you should consider opportunities carefully is that some work can in itself change your thinking as to what is important in your life. Some job opportunities can open vistas you never imagined before. Also, you personally may have changed since drawing up your list of what's important, and a new opportunity could force a re-evaluation of how you are doing.

There may be certain factors in your present position that would definitely make somewhere else better for you. It could be the people you work with, the duties, the work climate, lack of advancement opportunity, or any of a hundred things. Whatever the cause, you know it's time for you to try your fortunes elsewhere. If that's the case, you should go through the same kind of internal process first. List what it's all about; what you like and dislike; what your career objective is; why you want to move.

Your wife can help you here too. Playing your reasoning off on her can do much to clarify in your own mind the root of your dissatisfaction, just how important it is and the chance that it can be overcome elsewhere. If you've had the right kind of communication in your marriage, if you've shared your trials, your tribulations, your triumphs, and your dreams, she will provide great insight. She might help you see that an interim move is advisable if the reasons are right. The secret is knowing they are.

You've got to be honest about whether it's the job that's pushing you or yourself. This is something you must learn if you are ever going to find what it is that you're looking for. It's hard to be objective, but you must. You will never be satisfied if you continually blame outside circumstances when your dissatisfactions are really self-induced. Have your wife help you find things you may be blind to.

Another crucial element in your decision is knowing whether it will help or hurt your career. This could be the determining criterion. Let's say the job you have is all right and you're not particularly dissatisfied. Ask yourself what potential there is for you in the new job if you do take it and make the move. Will it be an eventual dead end or another step in the direction you want to go? Consider what happens to your career if you *don't* take the offer. Is it the kind of chance that could go either way? Or would it not make any difference? Are you tempted because everything is good, but hesitant because it's a treading-water kind of move?

If the move will have a neutral effect, don't go. If it's counter to your long-range goal and only appeals because of some sensational short-term advantage, ignore it. If you think there's a possible potential but no one else agrees, don't go unless you know something they don't. If there are possibilities that others you respect see, lean that way.

By considering all factors thoroughly your decision will be that much more solid. You can deal from strength rather than weakness and not be forced into a hasty decision. Go where you think it will profit your career the greatest—with one very large proviso: your career must be balanced against your marriage.

When you're sure that it's the right move for your career, it is that much easier for your wife and family to accept. But if there's the slightest doubt or uncertainty in your mind, the implications for your marriage carry more weight. You must talk it over anyway, and your uncertainty demands that you and your wife share in the evaluation process.

Of course, the first reason you should talk over a career change with your wife is to get her sound advice. It's all very well to write things down and reason and ponder, but doing it by yourself has definite limits. Your wife will help to pick out the soft points of your thinking, strengthen the positive aspects, and help you to identify areas that need further pursuit.

By having already shared in determining what's important, collectively and individually, this analysis will flow more naturally and easily. And while you should seek the advice and thinking of others you respect, there's none as close or honest as your wife. She will help you get to the meat of the problems that really matter to you both.

It will also be necessary for you and your wife to review your marriage goals in relation to the new job. See how it would affect what you have already avowed and whether you should change your goals if the opportunity is particularly attractive. Your marriage goals were set after some serious soul searching and you probably won't want to change them on a whim. Besides, having evaluated your marriage goals side by side, looking at them again can only help to bring an anticipated move into better perspective.

Don't forget her ambition, either. It may or may not be a major factor, but you must consciously make that determination. Remember, to be totally successful in marriage you must try to satisfy the dreams of both you and your wife. Maybe it's not so much a question of ambition but of basic values. Even so, you still must take them into account.

And be prepared to be surprised. As well as you think you know her, she could be totally in favor of the move even though you were sure she'd be dead set against it. With a continuing dialog you will have a pretty good idea of her thinking, but you can never be certain until you actually consult with her. Her decision will be based on many things, ranging from her own preferences to what she thinks is best for you.

A great part of her concern is the effect the move will have on your family—and this should be a concern of yours too. If you're happy in job and marriage chances are your children will be happy also. They may grumble about leaving school, but you must remember that your day is now and that theirs is yet to come. However, there may be extenuating circumstances, such as the need to be close to certain kinds of educational or medical facilities. The ages of your children should influence your decision, just as your own age should. Both you and they are more flexible when younger. You can make new friends easier then and there's a sense of adventure about moving. It gets tougher when you get older. It's harder to say goodbye, you're a little slower to adjust, and the new people you meet don't seem so accessible.

As for your children, certain ages are more critical than others. A move is not so hard on them when they are in the lower elementary grades, but high school is a different matter. You can't say absolutely that you won't move when they are older, but then you should be that much surer that it is necessary. When your children reach eighth or ninth grade they need the security of familiar friends and places and the thought of moving at that time is often worse than the move itself. But the last two years of high school are critical. You can hurt your sons and daughters seriously and in many ways by forcing them to move then.

You can pooh-pooh this and say it doesn't matter, but it does. Sure they can and will adjust, but a move at that time borders on rank insensitivity, if not cruelty. So no matter how obedient and good-willed your child is, your responsibility as a parent demands that you become aware of the implications, especially for the older students. It's still your decision to make, and you might choose to move even after considering that your child will be a senior. But just make sure you know what you're doing.

Of course, even the best child may rebel or resist. If so, you must stand ready to understand and help him or her to cope with the change. You must remember that your offspring has a valid point; he or she is not being ornery or hateful in not embracing the move. Nor is it a criminal act if you decide to let the youngster suffer a bit—you must follow your own star—but if you are uncertain as to whether it really is your star, you definitely must consider how your children would be affected. In deciding, then, involve your children. Explain the situation as thoroughly as you can. Let them know they are an important part of the process and that you are concerned for their well-being too.

In considering a move you must also think of the strength of your ties with home. There's been a tendency to ignore these pulls in our mobile society and often it seems as though everyone is a transient. It's not uncommon to have members of the same family scattered throughout the states, or even around the world. Lately many people have begun to reaffirm the need for roots, and many are being drawn back to the home area of either the wife or husband. Many have found the world wanting while others are less inclined to even go for a look. If you have these sentiments, see how heavy is the pull of staying close to home. If the significance for your career isn't that great, perhaps your desire to stay will decide things for you.

If a new job offer seems attractive but you still find reasons not to move, consider why you have doubts. Perhaps in your personal scheme of things your career is not at all that important. Perhaps you reserve top billing for other things, such as time with the family or leisure to pursue a hobby. While you still want a meaningful career you may be willing to relegate it to second place. Perhaps you've experienced a subconcious realignment of what's important and don't even know it. There's nothing wrong with that; indeed, you're fortunate if you can zero in on what it is you're really after in life. But you must realize that these are your true feelings and not pine away for what you really don't want.

Or if you find a place you like more than any other you can consider the move to be temporary. There's no reason it has to be forever, especially if you think and plan ahead. A move might be made now only to help you on down the line. Perhaps your wife's ambition can be fulfilled where you are now but she feels it can wait; maybe you've found the friends you want, but they will still be there when you return; it's where you want your children raised but they're so young it doesn't matter now; maybe your ultimate life-time career is there but a move now will strengthen it. The point is don't be afraid to leave a place you like when, by planning, you can come back when it's to your advantage.

While we're at it, what about ties and proximity to family, yours and hers? People like grandparents and aunts and uncles and cousins? Company transplants invariably miss their relatives, not necessarily mom and dad. View the move in light of whether it will take you closer to or farther from your favorite relatives and how important that is to you.

Then there's the matter of lifestyles, which vary considerably in different parts of the country. How will you and your family fit in? You'd better consider this, because although people are pretty much the same individually, collectively there are definite differences. Would you be going to a kind of lifestyle you know you'll enjoy? Is it rural or urban, and which are you? What about the climate? It's not a question of whether you can adjust but whether you want to. Is it going to be a good or bad experience? Is it worth it to you and your family? Does the pull of the job outweigh these considerations? There are many, many factors to be considered when contemplating a move. It's imperative that you look at all of them. You may never be absolutely sure it's right, but if you're careful and work at it, you can come very close to judging correctly.

Money

There is one determinant so important in deciding whether to move or not that it deserves special consideration: money. It's a critical, crucial item, one that often inspires grievous misjudgments. When studying an opportunity to make more than they're earning now, people make a common mistake in looking at the increased income and forgetting higher expenditures. This is one area where you have to be careful in your figuring, for once you've made the move your new boss isn't likely to give in to your pleas of money shortages.

A common error is to ignore differences in living costs from area to area and town to town. The prime example is buying a house. If you have lived in your present one for more than a couple of years, you may be pleasantly surprised at how much it has appreciated in value. When you sell it you'll be rolling in cash, so you go confidently to your new location and anticipated mansion. There, however, you're likely to be in for a rude awakening. Chances are you will not be able to buy even the equivalent of what you gave up for the same money. And if you're getting a higher position you may be looking for more than you had, not the same or less.

In some parts of the country property values have gone completely out of sight, so you'd better know what you're getting into. An unexpected expenditure on a house can eat up your money in a hurry. Before accepting an offer, go to the new area and look around. The best way of finding out what you're heading for is to price-shop for a house without making a commitment. However, you must also realize that price is just part of the financial considerations in buying and in selling a house. Unless your new company pays the realty fees—and you should check—you're liable for the bill, which can be a healthy 6 or 7 percent of your total selling price, and that's still not counting all kinds of closing and finance charges on top of your down payment.

If it's a new house, you can't forget things like carpeting and lawns and shrubbery. The cost of utilities may be higher, too, depending on the size of the house and the climate. Taxes also can be significantly higher in the new area.

If you buy an older home, you must anticipate problems of air conditioning, roof leaks, painting, and hundreds of other unexpected repairs. Once it's your baby you pay the freight, which can be pretty heavy. These things may not be necessary and, in any case, may not dissuade you from buying an older home, but you must anticipate the possibilities.

Find out what your company will pay with regard to fees, moving expenses, motels, meals, and anything else that can be an out-of-pocket expense. Each item may not sound like much in itself, but they can add up to many thousands of dollars. Find out what moving is going to cost, for your own protection.

Though housing is the biggest expense item, there are

many others. There is a surprising difference in the cost of food from one part of the country to another. Your new job may require a lot more home entertaining for which there's no recompense. Or maybe you'll be required to entertain at a club in which your membership was paid but not your monthly expenses. And what about clothes? A new job may necessitate a whole new wardrobe for you and your wife and that can cost a bundle.

This brings up your standing in the community. How will you stack up where you're going as opposed to what your status is now, assuming it matters? How much money will it take to either retain or improve your status? What will moving do to your wife's position and what will that cost? How much time and money will you be expected to contribute to the social needs of the community?

It's okay to think you're the exception, that you can economize in certain areas, but there are things you cannot ignore. No matter your personal values, you must be realistic in what you will have to go along with. That being the case, will the extra money you'll have coming in cover it?

You may be one of the lucky few to whom money is not a significant consideration, either because of wealth or the fact that you and your family can tighten your collective belt. Or, if you have a commitment beyond materialism, perhaps you can do without what many feel they simply must have. If you can be fulfilled in this way, and your family will support you, you're truly blessed. It would be fortunate for all of us if we could consider any move without worrying about economic pressures. But in this fast-paced, ever-demanding modern world the simple life is rarely chosen. And, though you may not want to chase the almighty dollar, you do need an adequate income. That's the way it is, and it's something that must be contended with.

It's legitimate to question how you will fare on the money that is offered for you to move. You must question all factors, not because you are money hungry but because there are things you have to know. Perhaps you can live on love and dreams and the esthetics of your career, but your family cannot. Don't be afraid that your income will never be higher, because usually it will climb. The important thing is to know for sure.

Commuting and Travel Duties

There are many other factors that could make a new job in a new location more or less appealing. Take the simple one of travel time to and from work. It can take a big slice out of your day. If you have to commute any great distance, you can read or do homework to keep it from being a complete loss of time, but something else will suffer: time with the family. It also might entail added expense, such as buying and maintaining a car, paying train fares, or whatever. These do not take long to add up, so be wary.

Then there's overnight travel and excursions away from home. Is it required, and if so is it something you're willing to get into? If you're not accustomed to it you may not think one or two nights away from home a week sounds bad, but they add up in a hurry. Some marriages and people are badly hurt by frequent overnight trips, while others seem to get by. It's something to think about, because even the most understanding and supportive of wives can complain. If you're already traveling heavily now and contemplate cutting back, you also have to consider what that will do to the marriage. You might at first say it will improve it, but there will be new adjustments for you, your wife, and kids. Consider all the factors rather than accept the change blindly.

To move or not to move—whether it be a new job or a new town or both—is too critical a decision for you not to be prepared. You're cheating yourself if you do it by chance. A move could be the best thing in the world, but it can also be the worst. You owe it to yourself and wife and family to adequately think through the ramifications to avoid the latter.

Settling In

The usual thing to do when you make a physical move to a new job is to get going on it as soon as possible. You're anxious to start and your new co-workers are themselves anxious to have you start. Then you rather quickly become totally immersed in the job, getting acquainted, learning and doing—which is great! It's exactly as it should be from the standpoint of the company. But it's a woefully shortsighted approach if you leave your wife and children to fend for themselves while you lose yourself in the challenges of the new job. In fact, it's not only unfair, in time it's going to hurt you.

Take a page from your own history. In previous moves, when has your wife needed you the most? Why, right at first! That's when simple things which have never been problems for her are suddenly difficult to handle. That's when she starts calling and bothering you at the office more often than she really needs to. For some reason, she becomes a real pain, or at least very demanding. Surely you've noticed how some wives hound their husbands when they first land a new job. You may even think less of the man either because he misses a lot of work or lets his wife pester him too much. Later when you get to know him you find that the situation isn't bad at all. If you're honest, it's been the same with you, and although your wife did tough it out, she didn't have much fun doing it.

Often the husband feels right at home because of the new job, but the same doesn't hold true for the wife. Even though she may be invited to all kinds of social events, she is still faced with myriad chores and duties that can be overwhelming. It's not a question of coping—most company wives do that—it's a question of whether there's a better way.

It would be nice if the company had a policy of lending a helping hand in settling, but most firms don't. Many companies are becoming conscious of the problem, but the majority of employees who move still do it on their own. Then the husband goes to work right away and the wife gets the lonely, often tedious chore of making a new home. To do it, she needs you, only this takes time you can ill afford to spare.

So anticipate her wants. Plan for that time she needs. Do yourself, the company, and your wife a great favor by setting aside some time at the start of the job to help her get going. It's tough because it looks as though you can never find a spare moment, but it's not impossible. If necessary, make the arrangement a condition of the job before you take it. A new boss is always more susceptible to bargaining before you appear than after. If you stick by your guns, you can make a convincing case that this will allow you to do your work faster and better.

Then, having won some time to spend with your wife, use it. Help her with things like getting a place to live, a critical decision you should be in on anyway. You should have already laid the groundwork, shopped around, and decided what your absolute top dollar is. You need to discuss your wants concerning a house, starting with such unalterable considerations as family size. Next figure what you can afford and what options you would like to have.

Then consider something even more important—location. You can trade some of your design preferences to get the proper location. This has been proved many times over—the most splendid domicile is nothing if the location is wrong. There's no hard and fast rule on this. What's best for you depends on your children, your wife, how close you want to be to work, your neighbors, and so on. It's one thing if your wife needs the security of being close to you, or if your children are of an age where they need playmates, but it's something else if your wife feels secure and you have no children. Each situation is different and you must decide for yourself. The key to a successful move is that you do make these decisions consciously.

If you have children there is the question of schools. Depending on what part of the country you locate in, the neighborhood school simply may not exist. The old days where you lived within walking distance are just about gone and you had better check such things as the availability of buses. Or you may prefer, or feel forced, to send your kids to a private school. It's the thing to do in many areas, and it can get to be expensive. Even if the thought is distasteful, you'd better anticipate the possibility because it may not be as cut and dried as you think.

After your house is chosen, moving in and unpacking is the next hurdle. Professional movers are usually good, but they won't do everything, at least not more than they have to. Even to the most honest, time is money; thus you need to agree on exactly what will be done at unloading and hold them to it. Another thing you'd better get straight before the van comes is how you're going to pay. Many movers require a considerable deposit before they leave for your new location. There's usually no problem getting the mover to do what the contract says as long as you stand firm. But what often happens is that you get anxious to get rid of them, so you hurry them off, leaving yourself lots to do. It's terrific for your wife if you're there to help with the cleaning, the unpacking, the picture hanging, furniture rearranging, running errands, and the thousand other things that need doing. If you're not there, the workload can be overpowering for her.

Along with the unpacking comes learning your way around. It's important for your wife to be independent, but if she seems ill at ease, take the time to show her the town, make utility deposits, run errands, and get to know where things are. Strike a balance between helping her and helping her to help herself. All you're really doing is launching her; she'll find most of what she needs on her own. But aside from this it's surprising how by giving her your full attention, you can get a heck of a lot done in just a few days. Find out when the moving van will arrive so you can better plan your before and after time. Again, it's not a question of whether your wife can do it or not, but that it's the best thing for you and her as a team. Many wives have done it alone, but often this can result in demands on their husbands later.

Take your time moving in. You're in it together; you may as well work together. Mitigate what you can of this naturally upsetting and nerve-wracking experience for her and, in the long run, for you.

It Can Be Great

If it's approached properly and thought through, moving can be a real joy. It can be rewarding and challenging and invigorating if you do it for the right reasons. If you are pursuing something instead of just running; if you're not kidding yourself about what you're going toward; and if your wife fully supports your decision, it can be great for you and the entire family.

But a move does not always turn out that way. There is not automatic meeting of the minds between you and your wife about whether a move is best or not. It doesn't matter how close you are, how strong your friendship, or how tight your communication, there's no guarantee that you're going to agree. You are both going to suffer long, sleepless nights if one of you thinks you should move and the other thinks you shouldn't. It may finally come to a point where you unilaterally say, "We're going and that's it!"

With the right kind of marriage your wife will accede to your decision and go with you whether she believes in her heart that it's right or not. Even if she resists, chances are she will go along. Your wife is still the follower when the time comes that you have no choice but to follow your destiny. If that's the case, and you have thought it out, then do it!

Your children and wife will survive the dictum and the move, but now it's even more compelling that you help them get settled. Do as much as you can to show that even if you had to go against her will, she is very central to your life. Get her involved quickly. Help her establish some social contacts. Help her find other people who share her interests. Join a church; if necessary shop around, remembering that some factors can be more important than denomination.

Don't forget her once you have become involved. It takes work to keep your marriage as good for you both as it was before the move, but done right the act of moving can bring your whole family closer, with each member helping everybody else. Many times that's where the sustaining strength for all comes from. A move can generate an appreciation of family closeness, and you may be able to profit from a move by re-creating something you may have lost. In moving you can get to know the importance of family, learn how to support each other, know you're working for a common goal. You can find out how you all fit together in the midst of even the most demanding of relocations.

Look at each offer to move as a possible opportunity for

your career and your family, but do so with a critical eye. Don't jump too soon and don't be pushed. Decide first what you should know about the job and then find it out. Be realistic about the money and its true potential. Thoroughly review all the implications with and for your wife and children. Then take the time to ensure that the settling in goes as smoothly as possible.

6

Planning and making the best use of family time

TIME FLIES. Once gone, it can never be recaptured. You can never go back, and nowhere is this more apparent than when raising a family. If you haven't experienced this yet for yourself, there are plenty of people around who will vouch for it. Children come and go in but a heartbeat. Blink once and they have moved from infancy to grammar school and through high school to adulthood. And nowhere else is your own loss of opportunity so heartfelt. You probably know at least one parent who laments the loss of the children he never had time for and who now are grown up and gone.

It's especially sad because many of these people had been forewarned and still made the mistakes. Don't let it happen to you. Thinking you're immune to it will only make it happen with all the more certainty. The only way to prevent it is to be alert to the dangers and work to counteract them. And it's something you can't put off. You can't wait and still expect your children to be there when you are ready for them. Your children love you, but if you're not there when they need you, chances are that they will not be there when you need them.

Most of us know the story of the prodigal son who left home

rejecting his father and his father's values. But when the son returned the father rejoiced, killed the fatted calf, held a celebration, and welcomed the boy back with open arms. It's a great story with a happy ending.

Here's another story—of the prodigal father whose son was the apple of his eye. The problem was that the father had no time for the son. When the son wanted to go fishing, the father had no time; when he wanted to play ball, the father had no time; when he cried "Listen to me!" the father had no time. Eventually the son went his own way, got a job and a wife and a son of his own.

But the father started missing his son. He looked at the considerable material gains he had spent his life accumulating, and found something lacking. For some reason he and his wife had drifted apart, and he couldn't understand that, either. Everything he had done he had done for her and the son and yet now he was alone. With only one place to turn he went to the son whom he loved and now needed and said, "I've come; let's be father and son." But there wasn't the hint of a tear in the son's eye as he closed the door saying, "Sorry, dad, I don't have time."

Can you imagine yourself in this tragic picture? Who is the villain?—the father who thought that material things were the most important in life, or the son who hardened his heart against his father and found love somewhere else? Actually, neither is a villain; both are victims.

Of course, not all stories turn out that way. Many parents ignore children during the formative years and when they need them the children respond. It could be that you'll be lucky, too. But why take the chance? Why wait until it's too late to find companionship and love and enjoyment in your children? Why risk depriving yourself of the very real rewards that the family can give you?

Watching Your Children Grow

There is nothing in life that can give you and your wife more pleasure than your children as they grow and develop—

if you give them a chance. Parenthood means involvement with children from birth through all their lives. It may be hard to look that far ahead, but if it's done right, they'll be there for you to enjoy even when you're in your seventies and they are in their fifties.

But they will disappear—emotionally at least—if you are haphazard in your approach or unaware of your responsibilities as a parent. You and your wife must willingly and joyfully give them the time that's so critical. In deciding with your wife what's important, time with the family should have been high on the list. But inevitably it will be stacked up against time directed toward your career goals—goals that can be attained only through hard work and lots of time. Here again you are faced with strong competition for that irrecoverable commodity: time. You must parcel it out, assigning priorities here and there to get the maximum good for all. You must face facts—there's never going to be enough time for everything. You might think that later on things will settle down and then you'll have that time, but it doesn't work that way. If you let other priorities take over now, there will always be something of equal or greater importance all the way down the line.

You may think that now is when you have to concentrate on your job. You're in those years that really make the difference and you cannot afford to *not* give it your all. But take a quick look over your shoulder. You also felt you had to give it your all when you were just starting out, and you'll feel that way in the future, too. The job requirements never change from that standpoint. To do it right there are always strong, legitimate demands for your time. Therefore you must establish priorities right now in balancing your time. You must figure out how much there is to go around and then draw the line. It's not easy, but it's something you have to do. If you neglect your children for the job, you not only miss a lot now, you run the risk of losing them forever.

Judge for yourself, but weigh both sides carefully. Nothing grabs your heart like the with-all-his-might hug of a four-year-old. Nothing stirs pride like seeing your child blow out one more candle. Nothing compares with the contentment that comes from your very own offspring seeking warmth and security in snuggling close to you. There is nothing quite the same as those moments when you know you are the whole world to them. And precious indeed are the memories you carry with you, memories made better by sharing them with your wife. Precious memories you won't have if you don't take the time.

Perhaps it's hard for you to imagine that you could still be vital to them as they grow out of the cuddly stage and get awkward, gangly, cantankerous, confused. They eventually become subject to outside influences of teachers, friends, and of society, but that's when they need you even more. Beneath the surface they are still kids whose parents are the most important part of their world, unless the parents betray this love and trust or lose it by default. So often these other influences come to dominate only because the parents are too willing to let their offspring go their own way, not realizing or caring what is happening.

What too many parents forget is that in the face of outside pressures and influences adolescents need a solid base for a proper perspective. This can't suddenly come when the child is a teenager if he or she has been ignored for many years. Children need guidance all the way through life.

You can do your child and yourself a favor by, for example, going to see a grade school play in which your offspring has a part, even if it's just playing a tree. Have you ever considered such a thing? Have you ever thought of this as a legitimate reason to take off from work? What would you say to your boss, you wonder: "Bill, my kid's a tree in a school play. . . ." You'd hesitate, no doubt. Maybe for something important, but for a grade-school play?—mothers attend those; they're no place for daddies who have to work. You simply can't take time off for something that means so little.

But going can mean far more than you realize. There'll be some heart-stirring, but that is a minor reason. What really counts is that the child knows and your wife knows that they are important enough for you to leave the all-consuming job for awhile. You can't make all such affairs but you can hit some occasionally. And when you make the opportunity, even something as lowly as a school play can be well worth missing work for.

The point is, if you don't get into the habit of taking time out for your children when they're young, when will you start? Next year when you won't be so busy? Or when it's for some truly important occasion? You will never be able to go back and pick up exactly where you could have been. Therefore, build your relationship through the years so that the children will always know that you are there. For them life is a series of critical stages and they need to know they have you behind them throughout.

Too many parents make the mistake of not understanding this need until it's highly visible in the teen years. Then it's hard to become involved because the habit is not developed and teenagers especially require patience and hard work before they'll respond. Because it can be difficult to tell if they are responding, the parent throws up his hands and gives up, thus creating more problems all around.

In essence, parents need to take a page from the book of the college students of the late sixties who were questioning, among other things, the values of the consumer society. They couldn't see battling for material gain if there wasn't time for the more pleasurable things in life. They couldn't understand why their parents felt the need to scratch and keep on scratching. Never having really faced hunger or doing without, it was natural that they wonder why not pause along the way.

And while their experience made for a somewhat naive evaluation, they asked a good question. Why this headlong dash to success, if we lose our family that's so dear? We can't give ourselves over to them completely—there's still a livelihood to make and a career to pursue—but we shouldn't take them for granted, forgetting what we want out of the family. But remember, the dividend for you is that you will better enjoy your children, your wife, yourself, and everything about your life. It may be hard to see but it is vital to your whole being, now and in the future.

Relax and Enjoy

Now is a good time to step back and see how you and your family get along with each other. Do you like each other? Enjoy each other? Relax with each other? If your kids have a serious problem, do they come to you? Do you know this for sure? And if they do, do you snap at them and tell them not to bother you? Or do you understand and take the time they need? Do they think you are on their side and that you care? Do you treat them as real, individual human beings? Do you show that you're interested in them? That you love them?

And what do your children think of you? Do you know? Have you ever thought about it before? Are you comfortable with them? Can you get the full enjoyment you should from being with them? Do you talk with them as a matter of course? What are they like on the inside—happy or sad, secure or uncertain? How do they think you are on the inside?

These are all questions you should ask yourself, and if your responses are not to your liking, it's time to do something about it. The first step sounds simple, but for many it is not: convincing yourself that your kids are to be enjoyed. They can be great fun if you learn to relax with them. See that they are people in their own right. They are not buddies, exactly, but they do have many interests similar to yours. Then, as they develop new interests, expand yourself along with them, always keeping in mind that the most telling time is spent at home. That's where you really get to know them and where the true enjoyment comes.

But you can't fake it. Just as there should be no lying to your wife, there should be none to your children. Don't try to fool them, because they will see right through it. You don't have to be a superman, and knowing this can help you relax. They are willing to overlook your imperfections as long as you are really with them—in mind as well as body. Just giving your undivided attention makes up for a multitude of sins.

They have their faults and make mistakes, which is a normal part of maturing and developing. As a parent you should help to minimize and overcome these; and besides, you can't really relax with your children until you learn to take their deficiencies in stride. Growing entails highs and lows, good times and bad, with occasional inexplicable behavior. That's part of the learning process so don't overreact in your surprise and disappointment. With all of your experience, can you claim perfection? Well, neither can they, so learn to take their shortcomings as a matter of course.

This can be especially difficult with the first child, because it is the first with whom you learn what parenting is all about. Parents often get so tense over this child that they deny themselves full enjoyment. Ask a couple who had their first and second child several years apart. They'll invariably tell you that they enjoyed the second more because they weren't so busy making him or her the best in everything.

How about you and your oldest? Do you expect more and are you a bit harder on that one? Obviously you love the oldest as much as the others but the treatment is usually more demanding because you've yet to learn what's important in child raising and what is not. There's no reason you shouldn't have high expectations—your kids need that too—but they shouldn't be so high that your children never feel successful. You may really have that warm spot of pride in your heart but the child needs to feel it too.

Of course, not maintaining discipline and high expectations can hurt the child, for if you waffle, he'll think you don't care at all. But it doesn't have to be an either/or situation. You can have your high expectations and be demanding in your standards, and still relax with and enjoy your children.

It's a tremendous experience for a parent to have children mature to where you can really talk to each other. Your offspring will bring you a whole new awareness of the world, as well as remind you of what it meant to you when you were younger. Just as your wife has added a new dimension to your life, so will your children. If you want to share it—and it's really too rewarding not to—use that simple technique of communication: talking.

You will still have to be a parent. That's a permanent distinction, but it doesn't have to be a barrier. This is especially true as your children get older and their basic molding is behind them. Continue to influence their attitudes, but let them know you consider them enjoyable and that you like to be with them, as you'll no doubt genuinely feel at this point. Knowing that they can talk to you when they have the need is a great comfort. In the same way that you often need a listener, so do they.

One of the greatest lessons many parents fail to learn is that sometimes you can guide by listening where you can't by telling. Parents can get so wrapped up in doing the molding, in keeping the young from making mistakes, that they just preach, preach, preach. In return, the children tune them out. If you think lecturing is the way, step back a minute. When you were their age how did you take it? A lecture was no fun but if you found somebody willing to listen it was a whole different ballgame. The thing is, when you listen they eventually wind up telling you many of the things you've been trying to tell them. They don't understand everything, but they do understand a lot and they can work out the rest for themselves if you are there to listen. And it won't be all problems. If you have really close communication, there will be a wealth of pleasures and jewels coming your way. You may not want to hear it all, but you can't screen the bad things and still expect the good to flow.

Above all, relax. When you are on edge, too busy with other more important thoughts, they clam up. When that happens, you've as much as told them not to bother you—and don't worry, they won't. Don't tell them that either by action or attitude. If the kids are young, they're going to be noisy and rowdy and get on your nerves. However much you want to yell at them, learn to bite your tongue. Instead of resenting them, reacting violently, shutting them out, or demanding perfection, learn to relax.

If you find that impossible to do, you probably should review the way you and your wife agreed was the best way to raise your children. Are things going as planned? Were you realistic or are adjustments necessary? Why do the children set your teeth on edge? Is it their fault or yours? Are your priorities so mixed up that you are subconsciously begrudging the time that they take? Do you have a false sense of what children should and can be? Do you earnestly believe that the joys will come if you learn to relax?

It's generally the same with kids, no matter what their age. They demand much from you, but the giving is worth it. Learning to relax is not surrendering to their wants; they still need rules, and you have to establish them and expect compliance with them. Don't let the rowdy little ones throw you off, and don't rob yourself of the joy that comes from taking it easy with them. Channel their energies the best you can and plan your time with them.

When you come home don't demand immediate quiet, because this is simply not natural for children. Or if you have to have quiet on occasion, give them time to let off their steam. You are a mature adult and it's up to you to be accommodating. Kids will adapt if they know the rules, but you must occasionally ride herd to teach them. You can't equivocate or you will confuse them, but you can set up quiet times, noisy times, game times, and altogether relaxed times.

Very young children are marvelous fun if you're willing to spend the time with them and know how to get the most out of it. It's heartwarming and will bring you great moments in daddyism.

As the kids grow older, the ground rules change some, but the need to relax grows even more important. If you've been relaxed all along, you'll have no problem. But if you can't take it easy, you're not doing a proper job as a parent and you're not getting the full return. Maybe you feel that relaxing is not in your nature and you doubt that it's worth the time—but it really is. The only way to keep from missing and losing your children and regretting it forever is to enjoy them now. And this requires you to be the kind of person they can feel completely unselfconscious with.

Home Rules

The one great rule for home applies in all other aspects of life. You've heard of it whether you practice it or not. It's called the Golden Rule, and in this case it means you must treat your children the way you'd like to be treated. This is important because it sets the whole mood and temper of family life. Of course, there can be different interpretations of the rule. What it doesn't mean is that you should give, give, give and never correct and never expect certain courtesies. Treat your kids as you'd like them to treat you—with fairness, openness, honesty, amicability, and love. Simply set the tone yourself for the kind of atmosphere you want in your home.

It follows, then, that if you want a pleasant atmosphere, you must be pleasant yourself. Don't come home out of sorts, ready to snap your children's heads off. It's amazing how many good executives work patiently all day with their peers and subordinates—and insubordinates—and then become short-tempered when they get home. They act as if they can't wait to kick the dog—or the handiest child. They come in and growl and seem to hate everybody.

Eventually they get it out of their system, but by that time everybody else is in a bad mood. The man is ready for the good, jolly family time but now no one else is, so he snaps back or becomes sullen. Then the kids work themselves out of it, but since daddy is waspish again, the cycle starts all over. Everybody's feelings get hurt, and if you're the one who comes home that way, it's your fault, you're the culprit.

This is understandable to a degree. You have no options at work. Maybe you can blow up once in a while, but that's a luxury; for the most part you have to hold it in. You have to exercise patience and not blow your top no matter how much you may want to. But the tension has to come out sometimes, and the natural place is at home. You don't really mean anything by it and feel much better once you get it off your chest. Except it's not so nice for everyone else. Your family can be understanding, patient, compassionate, and loving, but there is a limit. They can only take so much before a negative reaction sets in. Don't let it happen at your house.

If your frustrations build up during the day, day after day, develop some way to get it out of your system before getting home. You can tell if you're going to arrive home sour, and when you see that happening, do a little work on yourself on the way home. Change your attitude and get in the right frame of mind before you get there. Figure out a good way to do this, even if it means spending a little time alone first or stopping for a drink with the boys. But use caution here. It's all too easy to turn one drink into two or more. This is no substitute for relaxation. Whatever you do, don't use that artificial crutch, if only because your children will catch on to it rather quickly.

It can work the other way too. You come home in a good mood but you're hit at the door with bitching or shouting or fighting and before long you pick up the mood. Then it passes, but you can't let it go. Everybody else has it out of his system, but you're mad and won't let go and the vicious cycle is going once again. Even though you didn't start it and feel blameless, you're hurting everyone if you don't stop it. You must be strong not to get involved, but don't succumb. All of us envision being the master of the perfect squelch, champion of the acid tongue. But that's exactly what the family does not need. Instead, exert a soothing influence. Listen to the wailing, complaints, and frustrations but don't make the situation worse by contributing to it. The homecoming may be temporarily unpleasant but that's not as fatal as your acid tongue could be. Don't take the blasts personally; your family needs to sound off just as you do sometimes. If you take umbrage the hurt will keep spreading, affecting all. You won't want to go home, they won't care whether you do, and it's too high a price to pay for simply not biting your tongue.

And when you spend time around the house, as on weekends or holidays, don't be a grouch. You may not like the idleness, you may be champing at the bit, but that is no reason to take it out on everyone. It may be particularly tough on the nerves if you're not around the children enough to know that they're sometimes noisy and bothersome. You may feel an overwhelming urge to snap and shout at them. But don't do that. Instead, turn their energy and your own restlessness into something constructive.

Do some chores around the house (and don't kid yourself that there aren't any) and involve the children. Don't shut them out. Let them be part of it. The young ones are inquisitive by nature and will pester you to death—if you take it that way. But don't. Explain what you're doing as you go along. Let them think they are helping, and you will all have a good time. If your kids are older they may need to be nudged, but though it's hard to tell, they enjoy working with you too. So wipe that idle-day-at-home frown off your face and do something the children can participate in.

There are other times when you need to watch your attitude. When you give in, for example, do it graciously. You know the situation: your wife or children want to do something that requires your presence; you don't want to, so you say no. They keep on asking and nagging and worrying you, but you hold your ground saying no, no, no, until finally you're worn down, overpowered, and you throw up your hands and shout, "All right!"

But it turns out to not be any fun for anyone because you begrudge what you're doing and it puts a pall on the whole day. When you sense that happening, it's better not to give the go-ahead than to ruin it for all. And if you know you're going to give in, why make them beg in the first place? You shouldn't be difficult with your family. That's no good for you and it's surely bad for them. You only end up feeling terrible because of it.

And how do you handle little annoyances around the house? Every marriage is hounded by them and they become worse the more children you have. Like borrowing your things and not putting them back. Or the old squeezing-the-toothpaste-in-the-middle routine. Or the clutter on the stairs, the disappearance of that last beer, your daughter sleeping in your last clean T-shirt, or having to wait for the bathroom and then fighting women's things soaking when you finally get to the sink. There are all kinds of complaints that you undoubtedly can add to the list.

It's frustrating! And doubly so if you're the only one who cares. It's enough to drive you right up a wall. So what are you to do about it? If you rant and rave and shout you'll grow an ulcer and probably upset the others temporarily, but do no real good. It's tough to accept, but these things aren't very serious if you don't make them so. You shouldn't give up in your efforts to have things the way you want them, but you should realize it's not a matter of life or death. Learn to take these little annoyances in stride, to relax in spite of them. Keep trying, but don't work yourself into a heart attack.

Vacations

Speaking of heart attacks, one way to have one in a hurry is to keep skipping your scheduled vacations. Everybody needs them and don't kid yourself by thinking you are an exception. You must get away and break your everyday routine in order to clear your mind and freshen your thinking. It's the same with your wife and children. They need a break too. They need some new sights and sounds to broaden their perspectives and add to their growth. In short, make sure you take the family on vacation.

One of the big drawbacks is that it can cost a lot of money. Often the time is not so hard to wrangle as the money. Anywhere you go it's going to cost, and even a small family can eat up your budget in a hurry. Of course, there are all kinds of institutions willing to lend you the money, but stay away from them if you can. Instead, start saving and budget according to what you earn. There are plenty of things you can afford, and if you do it right, it will be even more fun.

You can make the planning more enjoyable by turning it into a family project, getting everyone involved in figuring out what you want to do, where you want to do it, how you'll travel, and so on. On that basis each and every one in the family can contribute. They can even collect pennies and quarters and dollars in a jar where all can see the amount grow.

Then, together make a detailed plan. Watch the youngsters get excited about it. You might even consider letting everyone vote on carefully chosen alternatives, with you making any hard decisions. One trouble with many young people is that they are forced—or allowed—to make decisions they're not ready to make and really don't want to make. If they can be included in your decision-making process it will help them see what kind of input is needed, why certain decisions must be made, and why it is not always easy to choose.

For the purpose of planning, start with a family council. Don't be haphazard, because it's more fun if properly planned. Get the family to look at all the possibilities, maybe dreaming a little, but mostly being realistic. Start with known factors, like the date, and proceed from there. As the children grow older you'll have more and more conflicts, so you'll need to begin your planning earlier.

Another thing—plan to spend your family time in a way that is quite different from what you normally do at home.

Introduce some variety. Do something new or uncommon. Use the vacation to catch up with your children's lives. Let them see you relaxed—and make sure you are. It's no good if you keep the same pace as at home.

Allow some slack in your vacation schedule so you don't have to push, push, push. Don't try to set a coast-to-coast record, either. What began with such promise could wind up a nightmare if you bring all the high pressure along. You may be a mover who can get things done, but let your batteries recharge while you're with the family. If you've never done it, never allowed yourself the luxury, you don't know what you're missing. It's precious, so don't cheat yourself.

One way to both economize and avoid the ulcers of extensive travel is to look at what's close to home. Often people seek the exotic far away when there are enjoyments just as rewarding near by. It's natural to think you must travel the longer distance but it's not so. Investigate what's in the state and in your immediate area and you'll be surprised at what you find. There are almost certain to be state parks, lakes, historical areas, and zoos.

Another reason to investigate what's close is the opportunity it provides for a long family weekend. Throughout the year you can take what are in effect mini-vacations by making use of the three- and four-day holiday weekends. These are especially nice if you feel you can't get away for a week or two at a time, or if your vacation is automatically scheduled. Often there is no choice but to use the vacation to see grandparents, especially when the kids are young. These are nice times but they are not the same as freely choosing. It pays, then, to know what's close and use it for your long weekends.

And while most vacations should be for the family, don't be afraid to go on a special jaunt now and then with just your wife. The children can be amazingly understanding though they may shed a tear or two. Don't feel guilty; you *need* to get away once in a while. The children will survive, and besides, it's good for them to see mom and dad want to get away alone together. When you have the opportunity, then don't hesitate.

That's true with borrowing, too. You should try to stay within your resources for a vacation—unless you come upon the chance of a lifetime. There are some opportunities so rare they will never arise again, and which you feel you can't afford to miss. If you really think it's that one-time opportunity, forget the money and do it. Some experiences are beyond money.

A vacation is important and the way you spend it can do a lot for you and your family relations. Don't let the "can't affords" put a damper on you. It's nice to spend a lot, but you can work around that and have a whole lot of fun doing it. Everyone in the family can have a good time on a vacation no matter what you spend. Plan it together and get the most from your budget. And remember, when you finally go, go relaxed. Take your camera so you can continue to savor every vacation for years to come.

Free Your Mind

Another great benefit can accrue to you if you plan family time and observe it religiously. That's the ability to solve your problems by not thinking about them. Enjoying your family can do wonders for you in this respect. If you come home with a problem and then worry and worry, the solution may escape you. You can search and search, but for some reason the answer remains blocked. You keep going round and round and though it's imperative that you get the solution, no matter how hard you grapple nothing happens. Your conscious mind simply cannot perform. But if you're smart enough to let it, your subconscious mind may come up with an answer.

That's right. You can solve some problems more easily in your subconscious than in your conscious mind. The secret is to forget it, turn it over to your subconscious and let the work be done there. Man is just beginning to explore the tremendous problem-solving ability of the subconscious. When you push a problem out of your conscious mind, your subconscious cranks away unbeknownst to you until suddenly out comes the answer you've been looking for. Put that subconscious power to work at home, gaining both time and patience for your family. Discipline yourself when at home to think of your family first, no matter what kind of problem you have to solve. Concentrate on putting your worries out of your mind and let the part of your brain best equipped to handle the problem go to work.

Think of the tremendous boon this can be to you. Think how much easier it will be for you to relax if you get your problems off your mind. Think how much more you can enjoy your family. And use the same principle when bringing regular work home at night. Clear your mind completely and just enjoy being there, until it's time to work, and when you do get into it you'll have a clearer mind and a fresher perspective.

For that matter, you must not let your homework smother your family life. Sometimes you've no choice but if it gets to be frequent or every night you must act to protect your family time by deliberately setting a period aside to be with them. Make it sacred; don't let your work or your troubles or your hobby or your evening paper interfere with it. Because when you come right down to it, that's what life's all about. The company will always demand more if you let it. There will always be civic causes that you should support with your time. There will never be enough time to go around unless you schedule it. Your only true freedom will come when you allocate your time deliberately.

Similarly, you can't let the family monopolize your time, either. You should be fair to all the demands made upon you, and at the same time be flexible when you have to deal with special circumstances.

7

Proper care and feeding of the other half

A WOMAN is a very special kind of human being, a complex creature. It is often said that you will never figure a woman out and when you finally think you have, you learn how wrong you were. But women are what make life meaningful for most men, who generally find it impossible to be without one for long. In fact you begin to appreciate the true sacrifice monks make when you consider that they spend their lives without women, who, to the rest of us, are the wellspring of life.

Women are different from men, no matter what it's fashionable to say. It's not a question of better or worse, but different. That's the point that women's liberation has sometimes missed: equality is not sameness. It has nothing to do with one sex being superior. When all the similarities are summed up and individual quirks accounted for, men and women are still different.

What that means to you as a husband is that you must stand back sometimes and observe your relationship with your wife. You cannot assume everything affects her the same way it does you. You must realize the load she assumes is different from the burdens you carry. A woman is a wonderful mixture of contradictory qualities. She can be a tower of strength when necessary, with endurance far surpassing yours, and at the same time she brings a softness to the family making an otherwise stark existence not only bearable but enjoyable. A woman possesses a free spirit that a man seldom can completely dominate, and when he does it's his loss. History is filled with men who were, for all intents and purposes, the boss, men who could move the world but who meekly followed their spouses at home.

And in most families the wife does have the final word, whether the husband admits it or not. She is the one who exercises the most influence on the children, the one who ultimately puts into practice family decisions, the one who makes a house a home. And if the truth be known, within the bonds of a marriage, the wife usually carries a disproportionate share of the load. The old adage of woman's work never being done is all too true and has an even greater significance in a modern marriage. Women respond to the challenge, but husbands often fail to appreciate their contribution. And this ignorance is leading many husbands to a rude awakening.

When a husband fails to appreciate his wife and fails to notice what she does for him, why should she stick around? When she does stay, why would she keep doing anything? Women themselves are growing more aware of the importance of their contribution, and the man who is wise, who wants to hold on to his wife, had best become aware of it. Not that there is going to be a mass revolt or a walking out by wives. The feminist call to arms has been met with a notable lack of response, indicating that wives are not about to run en masse from their homes. On the other hand, the women's movement has served to uncover a simmering dissatisfaction. More and more women are disturbed about their part in their marriage. They are coming up with some valid questions on what it's all about, what they are and aren't getting in return.

As women have moved into the outside world, earning part of the family income, taking care of the family business, they are gaining a sense of self-worth. It's only logical for them to wonder if they may be getting the short end of the stick. What is surprising, perhaps, is that they don't seem to mind contributing; what they do mind is not being appreciated for it. They are willing to shoulder the burden, but at the same time they feel they should have real acknowledgment.

That acknowledgment must come from the husband. Children can't really appreciate their mother, because they have no basis for comparison. So it falls to the husband. Occasional thanks are a must, but are simply not enough. You have to show your wife what you feel for her and how you appreciate her through your actions, by the way you live. Whatever she responds to, whatever she needs, that is what you must give her.

And never forget the practical side. Although you should be primarily concerned for your wife because of your love for her, there is a very practical, even selfish, reason to nurture her. She is the center of everything; as she goes, so go you and your family. You don't want to be mercenary, but when your wife quits or slows down, everyone in the family, and especially you, hurts. You don't realize just how dependent you are unless she's no longer there to lean on. Let her get sick or go away for a visit, and you'll start pulling your hair out in a hurry as you try to take over her tasks. Take care of your wife so she can take care of you.

Look at the difference it makes to you on the job. When you come home you want to relax and enjoy your family. If your wife takes care of the details of daily living, it can take a heck of a load off your back. But your wife doesn't operate in a vacuum, and pressures get to her sometimes. When that happens you must be there to lend support and sympathy. You must be there when she needs you. If you wait to give that support until she's completely down, physically or mentally, you're asking for trouble.

Besides, it's unfair to pile more and more on her, taking her for granted and assuming she is so strong she never needs help or relief. She's too valuable for you to neglect through your ignorance or lack of appreciation. Take pains to keep her as you should. Your wife will be stronger, your marriage will be better, and you'll be the one who really gains.

If Your Wife Works

Can you picture yourself with an apron, busily performing domestic chores around the house and kitchen? No way, you say—that's woman's work and always will be. The only time she'll catch you in the kitchen is if the table is set for a meal. You stand on the traditional belief that there are certain things for each marriage partner and the housework is reserved for the wife.

Well, you'd be right if you were living 50 or 100 years ago, but it's not that way anymore, because more and more wives have two jobs. One is that of homemaker and the other is that of income supplementer. Each of these jobs can be fulltime in its own right, and when they are combined it can be a very substantial workload.

Saying she is an income supplementer is misleading, too. We're really talking about income that is needed for living purposes. If you didn't have it, you would have to tighten your belt considerably and do without a lot of things, things that used to be luxuries but are now part of everyday basic living. For many families the only way to make ends meet, to enjoy a decent standard of living, is for both husband and wife to work. During the last few years the number of households where both husband and wife hold jobs has increased tremendously, and it is now at the point where to not have both parties working is the exception. It's a fact of economic life that the cost of a decent living is outrageous.

It's time to rethink the roles of husband and wife regarding employment. The historical division of duties is no longer valid, because economics has forced a great imbalance. While it's questionable if the duties were ever equal, it has certainly tended to overload the female when both work at outside jobs.

Being fair, it seems unreasonable to expect the wife to carry two full-time jobs by herself. It's downright shortsighted, mean, and selfish. Even if your salary is larger, it's unfair. The fact is you *do* need what she's bringing in and you also need her to do the lion's share of the homemaking. Only, she shouldn't have to do it all. Be practical. If your wife works day and night and weekends just to stay even with her duties, she'll eventually lose strength. The weaker she is, the more subject to illness. If she's sick she can't work, and if she can't work there's no income and there'll be an increase in expenditures. It's only pragmatic, then, to lift her load some.

But that's just a minor part of it. You should share her home duties because you want to, because it's right, because you love her. You should understand just how much there is to housework. If you've never done any, it's easy to underappreciate what is involved. It's a full-time, tiring job, and if you add a regular 40-hour work week—which is enough in itself to wear a person down—you can see just how heavy a load she has. If you're any kind of human being, you can't honestly say you want her to carry that load all by herself. There's nothing manly about taking advantage of her.

Furthermore there is nothing demeaning about doing honest work, even if it's in the home and has been traditionally reserved for the woman. One sure way to gain appreciation of what it takes to keep a home running is doing housework yourself. It wouldn't be long before you'd see that many of the things you took for granted aren't all that easy. By trying just some of the simpler jobs, and doing them right, you'll find there's more to them than meets the eye.

Offer to help your wife around the house. Share her load where you can. Don't be worried about your male image; the real man rises to the occasion and will not let outmoded, narrow thinking and prejudices stop him. Besides, there are many things you won't be able to do very well. Your wife is really better suited for some jobs that you'd be all thumbs at. But the ones you will be able to do won't seem so bad. And, rather than rob you of your manhood, in her eyes it will increase your stature and strengthen your marriage.

Don't plunge in like a bull in a china shop—you can make work for her that way rather than alleviate it. Talk it over with her first. Find out where she can use help most. You'll probably have to start with mundane chores, but why not? These are usually the easiest, and your goal, after all, is to lighten her load. The result will be well worth whatever you have to do. Your marriage will be better and your wife will be happier and no longer too tired to do things with you. You'll get a great sense of satisfaction and worth out of what you're doing— which is proving your love and accepting your rightful share of the daily burden.

If She Doesn't Work

This section should read, "If your wife doesn't have an outside job," because there are few housewives who don't work and work hard *at home*. Even with household help it's a big job keeping up with everything and running the house the way it should be. On the one hand your wife's staying at home should relieve *you* of the household chores, as she should be able to handle virtually all of the routine by herself. There might be occasional special projects or heavy things to move, but for the most part you're free.

Another advantage is that she can pay more attention to you. When you come home at night she can listen to you and pamper you a little bit. There's no reason she can't sneak off during the day once in a while and meet you for lunch. Her not working outside will almost certainly be good for the children. She can stay at home with them while they are young and, when they are older, be there when they get back from school. It's great for the children and great for you, because with their needs taken care of, they're happier and more pleasant to be around. Finally, it's good for your wife because she doesn't have the exhausting drain of two jobs. She can make and reserve time that is all her own. This, in turn, will make her more relaxed, a better, happier person. She'll have time to sip coffee with her friends, time to just plain enjoy life.

Sounds idyllic, doesn't it? What more could a woman want? She doesn't have to go and fight a daily battle with the world. She has demands, but nothing she can't handle in stride, with time left over. What could be better? Nothing, if that were all there was to it; if every woman could be content with that; if it were, in fact, as easy to do as it is to write and read about. But it's not that simple. Sometimes there are little things missing, like the need to feel she is accomplishing something. It's hard to finish a cycle of tasks only to start the same thing over again. It's tough to begin the same grind each week knowing it's basically the same as the week before. Your wife knows that there is nothing particularly exciting about to happen to break the monotony; she knows there will be no real challenge; she knows this staying home business is not what it's cracked up to be.

And staying home with the children is not so easy or wonderful, either. They demand care and attention almost constantly, especially when they are babies. A mother has to be alert all the time then. It's bad enough with one, but with two small ones it can get pretty hectic, and when there are more, they can really be a handful. Nor does it improve much as they get older. The kinds of demands and needs change, but they are still there, still heavy and all-consuming. This can be demoralizing if the wife feels unappreciated. It's tough to keep going if there is no sign that those you are laboring for do not notice or care. Husbands and offspring are notorious about not showing their appreciation for the woman of the house.

And what of her ambitions? It's easy to dream about "some day," but it's hard to keep going when she questions that there will ever be a some day. She can feel her life rushing by now, today, this week, and she doesn't want to wait to grab hold of it. She can't see that she will have the chance later. She needs something tangible, and as much as she does for her husband and family, as hard as she knows she works, as much as she gives, it's hard for her to see any tangible results.

Today especially there can also be a certain amount of guilt about staying at home and not working, not adding income to the family coffers. No matter how well you're doing financially, if you're on the way up chances are that your finances are tight occasionally. Your spouse feels the pinch, she knows the tight spots. She also knows that many, probably most, of her friends work. The women in her same economic bracket are not staying home but are out working and contributing. You can laugh it off and tell her that that's the way you want it, but it's not so light a matter to her.

As her husband, you must realize these potential problems and work to counteract them. If you want your wife to be your comfort and joy, your lover, companion, and hostess, she must have the proper mental attitude and outlook on life. You must do your part to give her that strong mental outlook, to help her know her worth, to convince and keep her convinced that she is a real contributor, rather than a drain.

One thing that's imperative is to occasionally let her know how important she is to you and the family. Take the time to tell her how much you appreciate her, how much she does for all of you. Prompt your kids to do the same once in a while. But not too often—with kids, too much praise will cause her to suspect they were put up to it, and that they don't really mean it.

Encourage her to have some kind of outside interests. It's not that she doesn't have enough to do to keep busy, what with car pools, meals, and cleaning. But so much of that is not her own. And no matter how much she loves contributing, she just cannot give and give without having something of her own. What kind of future is there for her if she drains herself today for her children? Assuming she's successful in raising them, they'll still leave one day and she'll be left with nothing.

Strange as it may sound it can be harder on the wife who stays at home and tends to those duties exclusively than it is for those wives who work outside the home. One thing is for sure—the burden is heavy whichever way they go.

Pregnancy

One thing a man can probably never fully empathize with is pregnancy. You can be close to your wife, love her dearly, and even experience sympathetic labor pains, but the hardrock facts are that a man can never really, totally, understand what it's like. You can see some of the effects, the changes in personality, the quirks, and the downright craziness. Your wife says pregnancy is a wonderful experience and yet she doesn't always act that way. At times she becomes completely irrational, unpredictable, and impossible to please.

You try to understand what she's going through, but it's frustrating. You do your best to make her happy, to be agree-

able, to do what she wants, but nothing succeeds. The further
along she is, the worse it gets. She wakes you in the middle of
the night and sends you out for some exotic food or on some
urgent mission. You go willingly, lovingly, only to return and
receive not the thanks to which you are entitled, but the accusa-
tion that you didn't get what she wanted, and anyway, you were
crazy for going in the first place. She says that when she's in one
of those moods she can't be pleased so don't pay any attention to
her.

Comes the next night and the same scene. According to her
edict you don't pay any attention. Then she has a fit. It's very
perplexing. She's completely rational one minute but crying
inconsolably the next. She loves you for giving her the child
but seems to hate you for distorting her figure. She says she's
as big as a cow even before you can see any difference. And
then if you dare joke about her size, you're in big trouble. She
may poke fun at herself, but you can arouse considerable
wrath if you are indelicate, no matter how light you think your
remarks. It doesn't make any difference if the joke had been
shared before. This time she took it wrong and you're a heel
and you don't know why.

Many couples, wishing to avoid the one-sidedness of pregnancy, are taking steps to share the joys and vicissitudes. The
move to natural childbirth is a step in that direction. Couples
are preparing to be together during labor, with the husband
learning to assist, taking a greater part in the total process. You
may not want to go so far as having your child at home or
assisting in the actual delivery, but you really should consider
being in the hospital delivery room when the child is born.
Witnessing the birth of your very own offspring can be a tremendous experience for you and your wife. It gives her a feeling of unmatched security to think that you would want to share
that experience with her, and this one simple gesture will go a
long way toward making your marriage very special. The fact
that you'll do this for her will make her feel she's in a very
special category, that she means more to you than most wives
do to their husbands.

It's also a great experience that will do much for you. You
may hear what labor is like and the pains of giving birth, but

there is no way you as a man can really appreciate it unless you are present during delivery. If you witness a birth just once it will be much easier for you to forgive the normal flare-ups and inconsistencies she is prone to during pregnancy. Observing what your wife goes through to give you a child will leave you with infinite respect for her.

Whether you choose that route or not, it behooves you to remember that pregnancy is a very special time for your wife. That's when she urgently needs the extra security and understanding that only you can provide. She needs more reassurance, more patience on your part. You may think you're giving a lot, but that's nothing compared to what she is going through. Give that little bit extra that will help to see her through. She more than deserves it.

Sickness

Besides pregnancy there are other times when it's hard to empathize with your wife. Sometimes she will go through a period of great fatigue and a never-ending parade of complaints. It's especially tough for the male to understand, because through it all she looks good, carries her full load, and responds to the crises that occur. It doesn't make sense.

You may laugh, but women have very real fears that men know nothing about. Therefore, even though it seems she's worrying over nothing, those nothings can be all too real to her. Treat her and them accordingly. Listen and sympathize and don't lose your patience. Just because you don't react in the same way doesn't mean that she's over-reacting. Bear with her and support her even when it turns out she was wrong, and hope with all of your heart she's never right.

Something else you should realize about female ailments is that they are often an emotional outlet. When things bother your wife, when the world overpowers her, when she gets depressed, she will complain about her health. And often the physical symptoms are very real. Mental problems, however temporary, can cause real illnesses, and your wife needs your understanding to help her overcome them. Be up to the challenge of listening, sympathizing, and appearing to understand, even when you really don't.

Giving Attention

One of the many aspects of being a good husband is giving your wife her fair share of attention. The secret is not to set aside blocks of your time, but to give her time when it will do her the most good. Do it when she's down a little, when there's something bugging her.

Granted it's not always so cut and dried. You have many demands on your limited time. You do set aside a certain amount for her and your children, but there are limits as to what you can and should do if you are to take care of your other responsibilities. For the most part that's fine, but just as informal moments with your family are often the best, those odd times that just happen spontaneously can be the most important. She needs you when she needs you, and that's when you should respond. It's complicated, however, because she needs you other times, too, and you cannot give her your every waking minute. The only really good solution is to pay attention to her as a regular matter of course.

Take simple things like work aids for the home. How do you feel about those household appliances your wife wants but doesn't absolutely have to have? Do you consider something like a dishwasher as another extravagance designed to send you to the poor farm? Or do you see it as a vehicle for her emancipation, a tool to give her one more ounce of freedom?

It may be hard to see it that way when money is tight, especially when she seems to be doing just fine the way things are. After all, she already has a washer and dryer and vacuum—and you can understand all of those—but a dishwasher? If that's your attitude, you'd better examine what kind of attention you're paying her. You should not only lean her way, but anticipate her desires and look for ways to make her life easier. That's the kind of attention you ought to pay her. It's an uncommon characteristic, but a good one to cultivate.

Yet another kind of attention your wife needs is when things around the house malfunction or break. These items are usually not critical, but are annoying if they stay in disrepair. They may not mean much to you because you don't normally use them, but she does, and if you care for her you will take care of them. Often they are little things she can fix herself, and would fix if you were off to war, but they're the kinds of things she becomes very unsure about when you're there.

Pay attention to her and mend these things when they get broken. If the leg of a chair breaks, don't let it wait. If a light bulb goes out, replace it as soon as you possibly can. If something needs a repairman, call one right away. You may attach little importance to these things because they don't bug you, but the fact that they are important to her means you should give them your attention.

And don't forget *inattention* when it's required. Inattention to little things that aren't all that serious but which you don't really like about your wife, the kinds of things that get on your nerves for no real reason. These can be mannerisms or habits or sayings or whatever. If you let them bother you, you're going to start reacting to them and probably not very nicely.

Don't let that happen. If she's doing something that gets on your nerves, try to dissuade her from doing whatever it is as tactfully as you can. If it doesn't really bother you and it will be a big hassle getting her out of the habit, ignore it and maybe she'll do the same for you with your bad traits. If she does something that you absolutely can't stand and the subtle route doesn't work, then talk it over with her. Try to do it without hurting her feelings, but whatever you do, get the annoyances out of the way for your own good.

To treat your wife properly you need to pay attention to her, the right kind of attention. Giving it to her in as many ways as possible will help you learn the total dimensions of your wife. You will be stronger all the way around in your marriage, because attention is what a true friend would give, what someone who really communicates would give, and most importantly, what a good husband would give.

8

Rights, freedoms, and responsibilities

WITH ALL THE REWARDS that marriage promises, with all there is to be gained, you may still find yourself wondering whether you are really going to get that much out of being wedded. You admit that it's good to give your all to the job; good to give your all to your wife and children. But what about you? After giving so much, what's left over for you?

And how about your wife? Maybe she feels the same way. Here she works from sunup to sundown for you and the family. She's there to support you, to be your friend, your listener, your critic, and every so often your hostess. She's glad to do it, it's part of her fulfillment, but there comes a time when she yearns for time to spend by herself, all alone. A time when she doesn't have to contribute anything. Maybe she even feels guilty wanting it—here she has a good husband, lovely children, a comfortable home; she's needed, she lives a full life . . . but she still wants that private moment all alone.

And she should have it. You should make it your business to see that she does; and while you're at it steal some quiet moments yourself. Everybody needs some unaccounted-for time. Time to do what they want, with no worries or demands from anyone else. No matter how loved and rewarded you and she may feel, you both have to collar that extra minute.

Now maybe you don't really *have* to. But if you never make the opportunity, both you and your wife can eventually lose your sparkle. It probably won't be apparent initially but it'll happen, slowly and surely, and somewhere down the line it will show up. You can see it in yourself when you get overloaded and have no time to let up the strain. It's the same with her. If she's always under the gun, she's bound to lose her fine edge. If it hasn't happened to you, you've surely seen it in some of your contemporaries. The change is gradual, almost imperceptible, but they wake up one day and that sharpness they once had is gone and what they once took in stride becomes formidable.

Contrast that with the fellow who grows in ability and strength, but at a much less frenzied pace. He puts in the long hours, too, but he also deliberately sets some personal time aside. It can be daily or on weekends or monthly or quarterly. He gives his all for a certain period, but when it comes time for his personal break, he takes it.

Or instead of a break these men use a change of pace. They do things at a different intensity, varying the pattern so as not to burn themselves out in any one segment of life. They have the capacity for working without hurrying; they take their vacation no matter the pressures. And, interestingly, they keep getting better, doing more, and getting promoted, all because they take care of themselves.

Take a lesson from them in terms of your job and your marriage. Those who burn themselves out don't realize the necessity of personal time, whereas those who keep going take advantage of and jealously guard their private moments. And when the point finally sinks in, your main concern should be helping your wife find that personal time for herself.

Let's face it. Once you learn the ropes there is always some way you can find your own time on the job. There's nothing dishonest or disreputable about it—you should take it for the good of the job—but if you need to, you can take a longer lunch hour; you can step out from the office for a little while; you can schedule that business trip out of town; you can take a break between the job and home; you can get away on Saturday mornings or weekday evenings. Your wife may not like it, but you can and should take a break.

Your wife has the same needs, but unfortunately she lacks your opportunities. She is tied to the house, more or less scheduling her time according to your requirements. So, if you have children she needs to be there for, if she must prepare meals every night, or if she has a job and must do the household chores on the weekends, the only way she can get away is if you cover for her. Your wife simply does not normally have the same options that are open to you. Even in this day of liberation it is unlikely that she can go out any night she pleases without careful planning. You may not object to her stepping out, but there are many things holding her back that you must help her overcome.

Every woman needs time to call her own if she is to keep her identity. In your pursuit of a good marriage, in your continual striving to get closer, in your desire to be together and do things together, you become more and more as one. But you are still two separate personalities, and it's vital that you retain that. The only way to do that is to set aside some time for her.

Don't kid yourself in thinking she doesn't need your help because she has plenty of time to herself during the day. It doesn't work that way. And don't worry about what she's going to do, because that isn't nearly as important as the fact that she be given the time to do it. Time she's responsible to no one for except herself. Time when she doesn't have to worry about car pools or children or being here or there. Time when she's free, for even brief periods, to do whatever she wants. She also needs to know that you want her to have that time. Don't arrange for it and then act as though she's betraying you in taking it.

Different Personalities

One of the most important things time will help your wife retain is her personality. There are many good aspects of sameness in marriage, but this precious quality of being different must be preserved. The two of you will never be completely alike, and you shouldn't want to be. Despite all your love and all your shared goals, your existence would be mighty drab if you were carbon copies of each other.

Since you don't want to be the same, you shouldn't want to dampen her spark of individuality. The more she's herself, the more you and your children will enjoy her. When she grows in her own right as she grows with you, she will be happier, more able to give of herself. If she can't grow personally, if you squelch her individuality, life has cheated her and you'll be cheated too.

She may perform the "motherly" and "wifely" duties through rote, but what gain is that? What makes it all worthwhile is that she is another thinking person with whom you can share. Only a fool would think that the activities involved in a marriage are more important than the spirit behind them. Living together as alive, thriving people is the secret of marriage, and you cannot afford to lose sight of that. If you get so wrapped up in the form of the institution, if you ignore the purpose of marriage, if you forget that your wife is a real person, then you are headed for disaster.

Beneath the routines of marriage your wife is alive. Her true self may remain unseen for years, but one day it will either burst forth or die. If it dies it's a sin, because you've suffocated something very dear. If it bursts forth there's no telling what direction it may take. She may well feel an urgent need to find herself, to live her own life no longer concerned with you and the family. It's a real tragedy if you let that happen. You can blame her and call her all kinds of names, but it doesn't make it any more her fault than yours. It doesn't erase the fact that you could have helped prevent it.

Do you see your wife as a person in her own right, apart from being an important ingredient in your marriage? Aside from such roles as your partner, your listener, your cook, your lover? All of these are necessary and must be present for you to have a successful marriage, and yet your wife is also much more: she is a free soul. You must maintain constant vigilance to prevent your relationship from becoming one dimensional. This requires believing in your heart that your wife is one with you, one beyond you, and one apart from and together with you all at the same time.

As she expands and fulfills herself, she will be that much more for you and the family. If she is forced to withdraw, to shrink her life's circle, she will be less of a woman to herself, have less to offer you. If you unknowingly demand her physical presence at the expense of her spirit, you may cause a wound from which she will never recover. It's critical that you see beyond the present and help her to escape the bondage that even a good marriage can become. You can be a good husband but still dull your marriage unintentionally. By seeing your spouse only as wife and mother, no matter how proud you may be of her, you limit her. By seeing her as a friend you have taken a great and necessary step, but if you fail to perceive the independent person beyond even that, there will be eventual erosion of your marriage's full potential.

It's not always easy for her to see what's happening when she's completely subjugated to you and the children. As crazy as it sounds, you may be too good a husband. You are her friend, you treat her right, you talk to her and try to be everything to her. But in the process her own needs for development are never realized. This will eventually suffocate her, along with your marriage. You'll still have a wife going through the motions, doing the routine perfectly, observing all the proper wifely rituals. But that vibrant lively person will be gone. The woman you could have had will no longer be there. You lose; she's lost.

Start now to prevent that from happening. Ensure that her personality is not swallowed up by the combined force of her husband and children, driving her to revolt some day or go completely under. Hard as it is to come by, make sure she has time to pursue the special things and friends that interest her and that contribute to her growth as an individual.

Fighting

One way to force individuality is to keep a steady battle going between you and your wife. You can pick on her to the point where she has to react. It may not be too pleasant for your family but it will sure enough keep her sharp. It'll keep you sharp, too, as you pick and push and jab and retort. It's great for the old corpuscles; it gets all the frustrations out of your system.

In fact fighting is such a good tonic, and there is so much of it in married life, that theories abound on how much good it can do for your marriage. They say it helps to get things out in the open instead of keeping them bottled up inside. And since clearing the air is healthy, husband and wife should fight for their own good.

This theory has been carried to the point where instruction books have been published on how to fight. Rules have been established so as to get the most out of fighting in marriage. The advocates even go so far as to show where the line must be drawn so that permanent damage is not done, so that the fighting, which may pervade all aspects of your marriage, doesn't get out of hand.

Preposterous, isn't it! How can you "kind of" fight with your wife? How can you have a knock-down, drag-out brawl and neither of you get hurt? Why would anyone want to live in a continual state of warfare?

The fact is, there's no way you can kind of fight—either you do or your don't. If you're not fighting, you're playing a game, and game-playing in a marriage is perhaps even more dangerous than fighting. There are lines which definitely should never be approached, let alone crossed. No matter how perfect the union and the partners, there is always something that can be dredged up or fabricated that delivers a real, damaging blow. And once that damage is done, there's no undoing. Little by little those damaging jabs and barbs add up. Maybe at first they don't do irreparable harm, but if they happen often enough or long enough they will. The time will come when you're going to fight too hard, and too hard is going to bring big trouble to the marriage.

You may not think you have any problem along these lines. You and your wife are happy and never have a cross word. You may kid her pretty hard at times but you don't really mean anything by it. She knows you're just teasing and so do the kids. Or do they? You'd better take a look at your kidding and what kind of things you kid about.

Is there a touchiness in your wife because of your poking fun that you haven't noticed until now? Does your wife still take your witticisms in the spirit that they are delivered? Does she come back with snappy rejoinders? Gay, lighthearted, witty? Or is there a bit of acid in her replies? Is she curt and cutting and sarcastic? Or does she not answer you at all? It could be she's trying to tell you something with her silence. But perhaps you really don't want an answer. Maybe you're really trying to hurt her a little? Not badly, of course, but a little. And maybe, if you think about it, she's trying to do the same to you occasionally—maybe not flagrantly, but with more than a hint.

Then you may be subject to a free-for-all round of insults. Wildly lashing tongues inflicting deep wounds and pain. There's no subtlety involved, just a brawl that barely stops short of physical poundings. You may even feel a strong urge to belt her. Well, don't give in to it. No matter how great the provocation, control yourself. Physical insults bring nothing but trouble.

Or maybe you're not bothered with bitter-sweet kidding, or knock-down drag-out fights, but you're nagged by a constant bickering. It seems as though you and your wife can't talk to each other without the discussion degenerating into personal insults. You start off as friends, but two sentences into the conversation and you're very politely at each other's throats. It's nothing either one of you want, but you can't seem to help yourselves. You both still consider yours a good, happy marriage, you still like and love one another, you are still friends, still working to have a successful marriage. But you just can't seem to carry on a decent conversation, and it's darn tough to live like that.

Any kind of constant fighting is discouraging and that's the big danger. You may call it heavy kidding, or venting your frustrations, but it all adds up to the same thing—an unpleasant situation that has the potential to get worse. At best it takes so much away from what the marriage can and should be that you cannot afford to let it continue. You can't expect perfect harmony but you can take steps to minimize the discord. Saying that fighting is a part of married life and there is nothing you can do about it is evading responsibility. Not only can you do something about it you must if you want to keep the marriage you have and want. By just giving in to fighting and getting used to it as a normal way of living, you have started the erosion process. If it's begun, or if it's been happening to you, it's time to do something about it.

The first step is being honest about whether you have a problem. You can't gloss over it and expect it to get any better, nor can you imagine you have one problem when you really have another and make things different, either. You must be realistic enough to expect to have occasional cross words. There's no way that a woman who has any kind of spunk—which you really admire—is never going to show it. Even if she regards you as lord and master, she's occasionally going to cross or criticize or question you. And there's no way that your self-control is going to keep you from sometimes saying or doing something you shouldn't. It's not in the cards for two people to live that close day in and day out and never exchange a cross word. In fact, if you never feel the urge to be contrary you'd better start wondering about that. Chances are, however, you'll never have that problem.

If there is an overabundance of criticism in your marriage, you must try to learn why. Look to see who's at fault, you or she. It's easy to blame her, but be honest. Is it because you've been having a string of bad days at the office? That she hits you with all her problems before you get any kind of chance to unwind? Are you worried about something, like money, and cannot be civil because of it? Or are you, deep down, really growing tired of her? Is it possible she's tiring of you? Perhaps you're consciously doing things to irritate her.

If you have a problem, go back to the basics of what's important to you both. Have you started to veer away from your agreed-upon values, or were they misleading in the first place? What's your attitude toward communication? Are you talking because you want to and because you are friends, or are you forcing it? If so, why? Are the children a problem? Are there unresolved differences in the way each of you think they should be handled? Is your wife overloaded with work? Perhaps she is so extended, and has been running around so much, that she's worn out and tired and cannot be anything but irritable. Maybe this description fits you even better. Maybe there's a high-pressure situation affecting one of you. Marital strife can be caused by any number of things, including life in general. Whatever is causing your battles, you've got to find it out and then work to correct it. No matter how seemingly innocent it starts, constant antagonism will have bad repercussions for your marriage.

When you do fight the inevitable fight, there are guidelines to keep in mind. Number one is never go for the jugular. Even if you have the ultimate weapon that would destroy her, don't use it—in the long run you're going to hurt yourself as much as you hurt her. The second thing to remember is never put her in a position where she is forced to use her ultimate weapon on you. Don't goad her too far just for the heck of it.

But if you do, and she goes to her knockout punch and staggers you, roll with it. Let her have her day. Don't, whatever you do, respond in kind. It's hard not to, but don't let that male ego of yours get in the way. If you do you'll come up the loser—there's no warmth in an empty bed. If you do get carried away and say things you shouldn't, and she says things she shouldn't, all is not lost. But it sure can make the path back to normalcy long and rocky.

The third and most important thing you should remember is when it's over—and you should get to this point as soon as possible—forget it, let it die. Don't hold a grudge and don't prevent her from making up to you. If you do, you're liable to start the whole mess all over again, and risk a really bad ending the next time. So get it behind you as quickly as possible. People are amazingly resilient, and any doomsday deliverance may not be so prophetic after all. But keeping the battle going will have it's price.

Maybe the experts are right when they say that fighting is healthy and good for a marriage. Maybe they're right to say it's normal and all you have to do is follow the right rules. Maybe, but too much simply can't be all *that* healthy. If you let it get out of hand it's bound to destroy your marriage, besides being unpleasant to live with.

Sex

As important as it is to get fighting out of marriage, it's that important to get sex into it. That's one of the great benefits of marriage, one that both you and your wife are supposed to enjoy. Everybody has needs and desires that are sex-related. That's the way we're made—it's inherent in the design of the human organism. Sex is great if you let it be.

But there are some things that sex is not. It's not separate from your total marital relationship. You can't fight like cats and dogs one minute and turn into amorous lovers the next. Many couples vow that other factors will not intrude on their sex life. They plan to keep it separate and apart from daily annoyances, only in practice they can't. There is no way you can neatly divide your life into compartments.

Sex is not a panacea for all of your marital problems. It would be nice if they could all be solved by a mad frolic in the sack, only it doesn't work that way. When you and your wife gain in years and have spent considerable time together, sex loses it's magic ability to make everything all right again. Instead of the ultimate statement of union between man and wife, it becomes a regular part of the marriage routine, still a super one, but no longer the main one.

Sex is not an all-consuming, every-minute-of-every-day force that dominates all marriages. This usually happens only if sex is lacking or when there are a lot of other things wrong. And even if everything else is as it should be, a married woman may not respond to her husband because she has grown dissatisfied with his bedroom performance.

This is not to say that a woman's interest in sex can be completely ignored, or that she won't get the urge for sex with or without her husband. One thing the current liberal social attitudes helped to bring out is the fact that women not only need sex, but are entitled to enjoy it. Sex is no longer considered a male prerogative, and there are few women left who feel guilty about wanting and enjoying sex. In fact, more and more women are becoming what is popularly termed aggressive in bed. But that's a misnomer. With the proper understanding in marriage, there's nothing at all aggressive about a woman making the first move. It's natural and healthy and beautiful when two people have a relationship where either one can make the first move. It's the kind of feeling you should enjoy with your wife. You ought to feel a thrill each and every time your wife instigates, because it's a sign of confidence in you and an indication that you're approaching the oneness you've been working for.

But a not-so-funny thing has happened in some of those marriages where the wife more often takes the initiative. The women are hearing the same excuses that traditionally they are supposed to have given. They hear about headaches and being too tired and not feeling well. Don't laugh—this is a reality in many, many marriages. Countless women are married to men who give so much to their work and day-to-day problems that they are just too tired to respond to their wives' needs. Is it happening to you?

Think hard now. Has your wife ever made overtures or let you know that she was ready for you to make them, and instead of responding you acted as though you were asleep so you wouldn't be bothered, or procrastinated going to bed because you knew she was in the mood but you weren't? Well, maybe you fooled her, but more than likely you did not.

It's time for you to take stock and ask yourself not how is *your* sex life, but how is your wife's? Look objectively at how you've been treating her needs. But remember, frequency isn't as important as timing. Sure it's nice to have lots of sex, but it just isn't always possible. There are so many factors involved that having sex every night or afternoon is not practical. But those factors must also be transcended when the need is there. When your wife's need is real, tired or not your duty is to satisfy her.

How do you measure up in this regard? Do you recognize the needs of your wife and are you committed to taking care of them? Or do you just assume you're on the same frequency—

when you're ready she's ready, and when you're not, she's not? Or if you do realize that you are on a different schedule, do you think it doesn't matter?—and matters less and less since you're not getting any younger? Don't think like that. Needs and drives are different, and if you feel your wife should only be aroused when you are, you're making a bad mistake. And if you don't think her needs matter when yours are on the wane, nothing could be further from the truth.

To repeat, sex is not the all of marriage, but it is an important part of it and one you should not deprive your wife of. If you do, you may drive her to an occasional search outside for the sexual satisfaction she's missing. While women with otherwise solid marriages are pretty well immune to being swept off their feet, more and more seem to be seeking temporary sex for the pure joy of it. You may say "Not my wife!" but we have begun to see that otherwise happy women are learning that sex with men other than their husbands won't mean the end of the world, after all.

They're finding that nothing changes at home despite their transgressions. The roof doesn't fall in and they do not have fits of hysteria. They still have the same family life, still take care of their husbands, still have the love of the children, but now their physical wants are finally being taken care of. It's not a pretty picture, and there's certainly no mass movement toward it, but this kind of thing is not uncommon any more.

By all means, don't neglect your wife and make her go that route. You may think it could never happen to you, and you may be right, but then, how well do you really know her? Are you sure of her sexual needs and how well you meet them? Not only in terms of quantity but also in terms of quality and variety? Maybe you've established the Wednesday night-Sunday afternoon routine, and now you're convinced that everything is as it should be.

But what about the luster, the sparkle, the freshness? Is it still there, or is your love making merely routine, even including the things you say? There's nothing wrong with a certain amount of sameness—it does make things easier for you both—but occasionally it gets a little boring. When that happens, does your wife feel free to suggest trying something different? Or would you think she is wanton, and wonder what's gotten into her? Would she just assume you'd be shocked and indignant and therefore not venture anything?

Likewise, have you ever considered introducing something new into your sex but didn't because you were afraid of her reaction? Afraid she'd wonder where you came up with it or what put the idea in your mind? Or do you think she'd be unresponsive? Well, she might wonder and she might be shocked, but if everything else is as it should be with you, it's an almost sure bet that she will respond.

Another old-fashioned notion that's getting the heave-ho is the idea that all there is to sex is the act itself, and that nice people don't enjoy the various preludes and offshoots of the sex act. They do, and you and your wife would, too, if you just leave behind the prejudices and inhibitions you picked up long ago.

Whatever your situation, make sure you don't neglect the sexual side of your marriage. Think about it honestly and don't be afraid to discuss it openly with your wife. You need to have strong communication, especially in such a sensitive area as sex. And should there be a problem, don't let your machismo get in the way of rectifying it. If it's serious enough, get professional help—there are many good counselors available. If it's not very serious and you can handle it yourself, do so. Do it for your wife, do it for yourself, and do it for your marriage. Sex may not be the only good thing in marriage, but it's good enough that both of you ought to be enjoying it.

Affairs

One phenomenon that many married men experience is that even as their sexual capacities wane or are already dormant in relation to their wives, they come to life with the possibility of an affair with a new woman. Strange indeed is this capacity to ignore the ready and able and loving sex at home while being unable to stay away from another woman.

Just as strange is the tendency to look for outside solace, blaming the wife's lack of understanding rather than honestly working to improve the marriage. All too often it seems that the easiest way out is to have an affair, to get someone who understands, who will provide the sorely needed comfort, make no demands, and provide complete relaxation. Someone who will give to you but not ask for anything in return.

It sounds good but it almost never is. You can't have the best of two worlds no matter how tempting it sounds or how much you delude yourself. It may seem to make life better for a while, but eventually it gets so complicated and demanding you can hardly stand it. There are no two people in the world who can enter into an emotional relationship and control it rationally. It's not possible, and no matter how intent you and the woman may think you are on controlling the situation, sooner or later it's going to control you. And when it does, you're going to hurt for sure. There have been legions of people who thought their situation would be different, but they all wound up learning the lesson the hard way.

From a practical standpoint there are two important commodities you're going to find in short supply when you have an affair—time and money. Of the two, money is probably simpler to overcome. You can start off easy, or she may live well enough that she doesn't need anything from you and doesn't want it. That's fine as long as it lasts, but many women who live alone aren't as well off financially as they seem. As you get to know her better, you find out about hidden problems and want to help her. You feel guilty if you don't, so you stretch yourself a little thin.

And if she's not single, or lives with someone else, you have no place to go except to borrow a friend's apartment, which is tough, or go to a motel or rent an apartment, and both of these cost plenty. If you're flush perhaps you can help her with her financial woes and keep the right kind of pad too, but some men have been stretched out so thin they've taken to falsifying expense accounts. It's terrible that a man could be pushed to such extremes, but desperate men do irrational things.

But even if money is no problem, time will be. At the beginning it's not such a hassle. With a little conniving, opportunities present themselves rather easily. Then after a little while things start to tighten up. It's not quite so easy to get away. Your children demand time, your wife demands time, your job demands time, and the woman you're having the affair with demands time. Don't think it won't happen that way. She may be content to sit and wait for a while, but the longer the affair continues, and the closer you become, the more she wants from you.

And where are you going to get the time to give? Only by stealing it from where you shouldn't. You can rationalize forever, but the brutal fact is that to have an affair, you're going to cheat somewhere. You'd better realize this before you get involved, because once in, it can be mighty sticky getting out.

Besides the practical considerations, there are the emotional aspects of an affair. If you think it's hard keeping one woman happy, think about doubling the problem, because that's exactly what you'd be faced with. Sure it's all lovely at the start, but that can't last. The "other woman" has needs too. She has real emotions and problems.

If your lover happens to be someone you work with, you're really loading the dice against yourself. There's no way it won't intrude on you at the office. Talk about circles! You've got a wife at home who you know you're giving a bum deal; then you start giving the job only half your effort; and finally you start giving your girl a bad time. Your life gets awfully complicated, and there's no way you can win.

Men often use the excuse that they didn't realize they were getting involved; they didn't mean for it to get out of hand, but somehow it did. Well, if it got out of control and you didn't see it coming, it was because you wanted it to. You may rationalize that you didn't want to hurt the woman's feelings and just couldn't turn her off, but that's never a real excuse. No matter if it's your secretary or your wife's best friend or your friend's wife, you can see it coming. The time to nip it is early. You can still be nice and friendly, but leave no mistake as to where your loyalities lie.

Believe this before you live it. An affair is no way to win anything. Instead of gaining, you're taking time and energy out of your marriage. Look instead at why you want to get mixed up with someone else in the first place. Is she so special? Or are you trying to prove something to yourself? Are you really dissatisfied with your home life? If so, diagnose the problem there. Is it your wife who is at fault or is it you? Or is it a middle-age grab for that one last chance at romance?

None of these are good enough reasons to lose what you have worked a lifetime to build. It's better by far to work to make your marriage the way it should be, no matter how long or tough a prospect that may appear. Sometimes, however, it may be more sensible to get out of your marriage altogether than subject your wife and children to the very real ugliness that could result. That's what an affair can easily result in, and once you get into one there is no guarantee how it's going to turn out.

Remember your responsibilities to, and the rights of, your wife. Give her the time she needs alone so she can maintain her individuality. Don't let your relationship be clouded by continual fighting. Be responsive to her sexual needs and don't make the deadly mistake of thinking an affair can solve your problems.

9

Be romantic

WITH ALL THE GOOD THINGS there are in marriage, it may still not be great unless it has one critical, often forgotten ingredient—romance. Yes, romance, because as many different hats as a wife must wear, she is first and foremost, above all else, a woman. And there's scarcely a woman alive who is not romantic somewhere in her nature. In the hectic rush of the day-to-day marriage, romance is frequently forgotten, which is a big mistake. It's important for a wife to know she is treasured not only for the duties she performs but because she is a woman.

One of the important movements today is a counter-movement against the extremist positions of women's libera-tion. Most women, it seems, believe in equality of ability, but they do not want to give up their very special place as women. Tough as women can be when pushed, most prefer to be softer, to have doors opened for them, to be given preferential social treatment. Many are concerned that in the rush for freedom they will lose more than they gain.

Women are unique treasures for men, and you should treat your wife like the precious jewel she is. That's all the reason you need: she is a woman, the woman you want to spend your life with. Let her know that you value her. You have made the commitment to a lifetime of togetherness, and you should show her that she's worth that commitment.

You may say your wife knows that you love and cherish her, but you've never had the time to be romantic. Maybe you're not comfortable with all that mushy stuff, and really don't know how to go about it anyway. Or your wife seems to get along fine without your being romantic and she wouldn't know how to act if you were. You and she are doing all right now, so why bother with something you're uncertain about? What's in it for you, anyway? That's good, solid, husbandly reasoning, and if that's your idea you have lots of company—lots of mistaken company.

In the first place, maybe your wife knows you love and cherish her and maybe she doesn't. Does she think you take her for granted? If you're honest with yourself, maybe you do. Even if deep down in her heart she knows you love her, she needs tangible reassurance. You can't express your love through mental telepathy or osmosis. You must actively communicate your feelings.

There are many ways of showing your love and devotion, and she understands that you have certain limitations along those lines. But you can make her feel a lot better if you not only go as far as you normally are capable, but make an occasional effort to go beyond that. Your wife may seem to be getting along without these attentions—she's probably learned she has no choice—but that doesn't mean that she wants to or should.

Don't worry about what you're going to get out of it. Your return will be more than ample. In any case, that should have nothing to do with your wanting to give as much as you can toward making your wife feel like a woman. Your motivation should be simply that she's worth it and deserves it. She's a woman and should be made to know that you appreciate and respect that fact.

If you accomplish that, you'll be amazed at what happens. Your wife will be transformed into a loving, attentive person. She'll start treating you as you want to be treated instead of just taking you for granted too. If you're honest with yourself, there are times when you feel kind of neglected. You know that she still loves and cares for you but it's not the same as when you were first married. She doesn't seem to be so concerned with your well-being and is not quite as demonstrative as she once was. It's probably not something you dwell on, but occasionally you do become momentarily wistful for what once was. No need to be wistful. Put romance into your marriage and what used to be can again be a reality.

Of course, your well-being should not be the main force behind treating your wife like a woman. It is a nice return, but it probably won't materialize if that is all that prompts you into being romantic. It's selfish, and the discerning wife will be only too aware of what you're doing and why. Going through the motions is never enough. For a real return, you have to be romantic because you want to be *for her*. Romance must come from your heart, even though at first the motivation begins in your mind. Stop and do some soul searching. Do you let your wife know that she is indeed precious to you? Do you regard her as the epitome of womanhood, which is so dear to you? Do you let her know that she is worth doing for simply because she is who she is?

If you do not, now is the time to start correcting the situation. It won't be an overnight accomplishment, but it can happen in a short time if you want it to. It depends a great deal on how committed you are, on whether you want romance or are only going through the motions. Of course, going through the motions is a start, and if you keep at it a strange thing is liable to happen: you'll start enjoying and wanting and believing in romance yourself. Your wife's response may be limited at first, but she will definitely take notice.

Understanding

Being romantic doesn't necessarily mean doing something. Indeed, one of the most effective ways of making your wife feel like a woman is to simply understand her as a woman, as a special human being.

This sounds easy, but it's really not. It requires patience, time, and empathy. You must be able to put yourself in her place because you know and appreciate that her place is unique. Your wife is subject to pressures and anguish that are unfamiliar to you, and it is vital to her to know that you realize this.

Understanding often just means being there when your wife needs you, even if the reason seems minor. To her it is not. Understanding means going along with her whims whether you can see their logic or not. In fact, a large part of understanding is going along with what is illogical to you. What you must remember is how it seems to her and not how it strikes you.

It's a fact of life that in many situations your wife's perspective will differ from yours. You should make the effort to see it from her viewpoint, to refrain from yelling and losing your cool because she doesn't agree with your way of looking at things, even when you're sure you know better. When she plagues you with questions that seem stupid and idiotic to you, you must remember that they are not stupid and idiotic to her. Don't blow up—understand. It's surprising how often her point is logical when seen from her perspective.

And when your wife is emotionally upset you should be especially understanding. Here's an area where men usually have little empathy because they try to apply their own reasoning where it does not fit. In trying to make rational what is an irrational situation, they only make things worse. When that happens and you are clearly out of your depth, it's crucial that you play the role of comforter rather than critic.

The key to understanding your wife is realizing that you're not going to understand, in the true sense of the word, exactly what it is you're supposed to understand. At the same time you must make her realize that you do understand in another sense. You know that a woman's emotions vary in cycles that are different from yours. You must also understand that your wife's surface strengths and failings may not be her real strengths and weaknesses. It's a complicated business; at the very least understand that there is depth to this wonderful woman who is your wife.

She will have many ups and downs that you will not share

but you must be sympathetic when she experiences these. You must keep cool when you do something innocent and she flies into a rage because of it. You must maintain your own perspective when you give her a compliment or gift and instead of being pleased she's disappointed. You must grasp the pressures of being a woman, mother, wife, and so much more all at once.

If she's upset about something and snaps at you instead, try to see what's behind it, and don't take her digs personally. Understand that she needs an outlet, just as you sometimes do. And you must keep in mind above all that she's only human. As hard as she tries she's still going to come up short sometimes. Those periods when you have to stand by her, knowing she has given her best, may be the hardest for you because it may be the most disappointing. And it is when she's tried her hardest, done her best, and knows she's failed herself and you, that you must really be there.

If she feels you're forgiving and understanding she'll try that much harder to keep from disappointing you again. But if she does, understand and forgive again and again. Even if you can't help getting mad and shouting, once you rid your system of it, then forget it. Have the kind of patience that comes from being strong.

There's no problem forgiving or understanding when your wife takes care of you the way you want her to, when she's exactly the kind of woman you want, when time alone does the healing. That's not understanding, and it won't make your wife know she's something special to you, or that you have kept up with what's going on in her mind and life. Understanding is one of the major touches that will set your marriage apart. Your wife will know that you're giving her more. She'll know that you have made the effort to understand her as a woman, the unique woman that she is.

Tenderness

When you truly grasp the beauty and wonder of your wife, you are on the path toward being an exceptional husband, for you will have a quality that is so needed in a marriage, that of tenderness. If you want to have a super wife, one who will go the extra mile time and again, try a little—a lot—of tenderness. There's not a woman alive who won't melt for a man who knows when to be tender. This one quality can make up for many of the normal grinds you and your wife experience together. This is the characteristic that separates husbands in fact from husbands in name.

Some husbands try. They provide for their wives, are loyal to them, love them, are friends to them, and communicate with them. On balance that's not a bad performance, but there is still that little extra bit that does so much more.

Unfortunately, it's the kind of thing many men are not very good at. They feel awkward, and probably they don't really believe tenderness is very important. Many "he-men" equate being tender with being soft, but they are not the same at all. And many men, far too many, never even think about it. If that's true about you, start now to consider what it is and what it means. If you're conscious of the need to be tender and give it a serious try, it's not difficult. Like understanding, tenderness is something that sets your marriage apart, that something extra a woman yearns for that makes her feel like a woman.

Being tender calls for sensitivity to your wife's moods and needs. It's more than understanding. It's being gentle and kind. It means the ability to sense her need for comfort and reassurance. It's letting her know you're there when she needs you. By being tender, you offer a security that tells her how much she really means to you.

How do you show tenderness? There are hundreds of ways, but it's primarily through attitude, an attitude that is conveyed by your touch, for one thing. Physical contact relays a feeling of rapport and signifies understanding. The magic quality of touching has been known through all the ages and can be an extremely useful tool in your husbandly repertoire.

Take your own experience. When you've been down, a simple touch by your wife or someone close has made you feel a whole lot better. The gesture showed that they knew how you felt, that they cared, and that they were there with you. It was doubly or trebly meaningful if that someone was a person you loved and by that touch showed that he or she loved you too. Think how effective such a technique can be in your everyday married life. It's such a simple thing to do, one you can handle without any threat to your masculinity and without fear of bumbling. Reach out to your wife. Lay your hand upon her so she can feel the strength, the support, the love, the tenderness you feel for her.

It's a wonder worker most of the time, but not always. Don't be offended if she pulls away. Sometimes your wife can get into such a state that she acts as though she doesn't want comfort or tenderness from anyone, especially you. Don't make the mistake of reacting in kind. That's when she needs you the most—and can show it the least. For you, those times may strongly tempt you to say, "Forget it, baby." You made the gesture, you tried to do what was right, you reached out in love and were rejected, so you won't bother to offer any more.

But that's wrong. Even if your gesture was rebuffed, you're wrong to let it set your heart and mind against her. If her emotions are in that much disarray she needs you more than ever, but it calls for a super effort on your part to give her the tenderness she has to have. When she turns away and you feel rebuffed, keep trying. Don't let your hurt sour your whole relationship. Work to overcome it. If you don't persevere, she may feel you didn't really mean the comfort you were extending. She will believe that despite her great need, you were just going through the motions and didn't care enough to follow through. This may not seem entirely logical, but emotions never are, and it's up to you to overcome these inconsistencies. The times you build your relationship the most are those when you give her what she needs even though it is painful for you to do so. If you really are easily put off, you might question whether you really do care. There is no challenge to being a fair-weather husband. When the going gets tough, demonstrate your staying power and she will know that you are there because of her.

Expressing tenderness should not be saved for special occasions. It's the best proof of your love when it's spontaneous and is consistently demonstrated.

Another good way to show your love is to pamper her. Show her just what a special place she has by doing things for her. Help her in her work by taking over part of it unexpect-edly. She may protest and tell you not to, but you can bet that she appreciates it. Do some unusual things for her, too, like bringing her dinner in bed. Lock her away from the kids and the telephone, fetch her favorite book or magazine, and serve her dinner yourself. Or some evening let her have the luxury of having to do nothing, of being by herself to do whatever she wants. It's impossible to do this every day, but doing it once in awhile will give her a tremendous uplift.

Wining and Dining

There's not a woman alive who doesn't occasionally want to be taken away from it all. Your wife probably doesn't mind the everyday work, but it sometimes gets to be too much. As an understanding husband, you should try to keep that from hap-pening by taking her away from it all before it overpowers her. Take her somewhere in a special way so she knows you are doing it for her and her alone. Do it in such a manner as to make it special without costing a fortune.

One excellent solution is to invite your wife out for a pri-vate, romantic evening. Just you and she, with no rush or hurry of any kind. Find a quiet restaurant with atmosphere where you can sit and enjoy each other. You might even make an intentional effort not to talk about problems. Keep the conver-sation light and uncomplicated, and if the mood starts turning homeward, steer it away deftly and persistently. Then make a night of it. Go dancing or see a play or a movie or whatever your wife prefers. The important thing is for her to know that this is her evening because she is special.

And don't make the mistake of thinking you can combine this with a family night out. You need some of those too, but they're definitely not the same. Don't give in to your wife if she says that a night out with the kids is fine. She not only deserves to have a romantic evening with you alone, she has to have one fairly often. As her husband you should be aware of that and schedule them without being prodded. Otherwise she'll think you felt you had to do it and that's not quite the same.

There's no set rule as to how often you should plan your romantic nights out. It's not always easy. There can be all kinds of conflicts with work; you have friends and social obligations and you need to spend some of your available time with your children, who have their own schedules to live by. When you consider all the other factors, time left over for you and her is not all that available. Nevertheless, if you give proper thought you can find the time. Take advantage of unexpected opportunities. If things break right and you have a chance you didn't anticipate, jump at it. Some of the best times for you and your wife are spontaneous, so grab them when you can.

In general, be alert to the special needs of your wife. If you come home and find that everything seems to have piled up on her that day, ask her out then and there before she explodes. Don't let it get to that stage; it's no fun for her either. When she seeks relief that way it's not because she wants to, but because she's under so much pressure she can't help herself. It's up to you to be flexible and to react and anticipate accordingly.

It's also more fun all around if you don't let it get to that point. You should have your nights out often enough so that your wife knows that they are coming and that they are something she can look forward to and count on. And you don't have to wait for a night out for candlelight and wine. Have a romantic evening at home. She will enjoy preparing an intimate meal and setting if she knows you'll enjoy sharing it with her.

That's really what being romantic comes back to—letting her know that you still think she's desirable, a woman you want to be intimate with. If you can make her feel desirable, if you can make her feel she has that extra something that makes you glow, you have the romantic touch.

There are other things you can do, such as sending your wife flowers regularly. Don't think about the expense, but about how much pleasure they will give her. And bring a bottle of wine home once in a while. Feed the kids early and then have dinner alone with her, even if it's just your regular fare. A standard meal can seem like exquisite cuisine if the children are out of the way, you've put your work aside, and you've cleared your mind to be totally with your wife.

If you make her think that this kind of evening appeals to you, you're well on your way toward re-establishing romance in your marriage. She'll think it's great you care that much about her. Occasionally, then, bring home a bottle of champagne for no reason except to share it with her. Do it with feeling and you'll see that romance isn't half bad.

Away Alone Together

Another ingredient necessary to the romantic package is you and your wife going away together. This calls for considerably more planning and money than a night on the town, but if it's done right, it's well worth the cost.

It's unrealistic in most cases to think about an exotic vacation spot, but if you look hard enough you'll find something close by. It may be in your own city, a neighboring town, or one a little farther away, but there is sure to be a good hotel featuring excellent entertainment within driving distance. Take your wife and check in for an evening. Enjoy a dinner, a show, and most importantly a night away together with nothing on your minds but each other. With the proper attitude you can do wonders for your marriage. But there are a few things to keep in mind.

First, leave your work and worries behind. You are not going to make your wife feel very important if, during your stay, you talk about and/or think about nothing but business. Once you get there, follow her lead. If you're a tennis buff but she hates the sport and would rather do something else, accommodate her. If you are a clock-watcher by nature but schedules are not important to her, bite your tongue and go her unhurried way for a change. If you abhor shopping but she wants to do some, go along with her. Devote your time to doing what she wants and being together.

Pamper her while you have this chance. It's not so easy to do in the course of the regular routine at home, so treat her extra nice when you are away. Give in to what she wants. Let her sleep late. Let her luxuriate in pure idleness if that's what she wants. Let her lounge around and have the pleasure of a leisurely late breakfast with you. There is something magical about breakfasting at a time your wife really wants it rather than when she has to have it. Even if you're starving and don't think you'll last another minute, hold off until the timing is right for her. Such moments can bring unparalleled closeness. And by all means, leave behind all newspapers and homework.

These unhurried and relaxed moments should be cherished; they are all too rare in the hectic pace of modern living. Like so many things in married life, if you do not realize their importance and plan for them, they will never happen. Now is the time to stop and evaluate how you measure up in this regard. You'll be surprised at how little there is to call your own.

Clothes

Of course, with all this going out, you just know that sooner or later your wife is going to complain that she doesn't have anything to wear. No matter how bulging those closets look to your jaundiced male eye, there's nothing suitable for her to be seen in. Her clothes may look pretty good to you, and you may still remember paying some pretty big bills. She may even have a new outfit that she hasn't worn yet. Still, she swears she has nothing to wear. She's not kidding. She's not trying to break you, or force bankruptcy. She definitely needs new clothes.

Clothes are special to a woman in a way they never are to a man. Even the most thrown-together, casual outfit takes a lot of thought and planning before your wife will wear it. She just can't slip on jeans and sweatshirt unless it is the right sweatshirt and the right pair of jeans. Even if the same outfit worked last week, it may not be right this week. Maybe that scarf is no good now, or her hair is different, or her skin tone is not the same, or a dozen other things beyond your comprehension are totally askew.

A woman dresses for a man. And that means you. But it must come out looking right according to her own standards. A woman must think she looks good in order to feel good. And as an astute husband you should notice that if your wife stops caring about her appearance, her hair, and dress, there is something drastically wrong or about to go wrong. So, instead of arguing and fighting about costs, compliment her on her style and taste. Help her find what suits her and encourage her to stay with that. There's always enough individuality within a style to accommodate the new while keeping her own distinctive flavor. Instead of sameness, she can create a unique blend that shows style and class all at the same time. Let her know you appreciate her ability to do that.

An added advantage is that she will get more mileage out of what she buys. She can purchase clothes to build on what she has, rather than completely change her wardrobe each new season. Too sharp a change can be disastrous from the standpoint of both money and looks. Your wife may not be suited to a wide range of styles and fads and thus may be better off sticking to what she knows is right for her.

When she shops this way, tell her she's doing well. Be lavish in your praise so that she knows she looks nice and doesn't have to compete in the fad world. Occasionally you may have to stretch a point to help her get out of the dumps. Also, you may not understand what she is trying to do. But if she does look bad and knows she looks bad, don't lie about it. Don't rub it in, but don't tell her she looks good when you really don't think she does.

And don't—although it's almost a certainty you won't— forget the cost of clothes. You want her to look nice and she has to buy some new things to do it. Since this is what you really want, don't act like an ogre when it happens. If there's no choice, why ruin it for her? And when you really want her to take something back because of cost, tell her diplomatically.

But it's occasionally worth it to splurge. If it's something extra special and you can swing it with a little sweat, do so. But don't let her get carried away if you really can't afford it. She's bound sometimes to want things that are simply out of the question. In refusing, you may be prompting a bucket of tears, but she will survive, especially if she knows you're fair and do your best when you can afford it.

To keep from disappointing her and to help her know just what the limits are, go over the budget with her and expect her to spend what's right and reasonable. With no let-up in inflation, it's hard to keep up, but you must make the effort. Let her know how much money you have set aside for her to spend on herself and then encourage her to spend it. Even the best shopper must replace what is worn out or is too far out of style. A budget will help two ways: it will give her the enjoyment of staying fashionable, knowing that you appreciate the satisfaction she gets from a new outfit; and by going along every year, you won't get hit for a whole new wardrobe all at once. Since it's going to have to be done anyway, you may as well let her have her fun.

Use clothes-buying to show your wife that you believe she deserves the best you can afford. Try to understand how important clothes are to her and let her know they are important to you too. When she looks nice, tell her she does. When she does something clever with something old and it looks sharp, notice it and tell her. Let her know you're proud of the way she looks. Let her know that as your woman she's worth every cent.

Special Occasions

There is one cardinal rule that a husband should never ignore. That's to never, ever, forget special occasions. This is one of the great sins many husbands commit without realizing how serious it is. Classically, women attach far more significance to occasions and their observance than men do. Women feel slighted if their husband is too busy to remember. It hurts them to have to remind their husbands that the occasion is coming or that it's today.

Husbands, on the other hand, seem to take almost perverse pleasure in forgetting such things as anniversaries, birthdays, or their own special occasions. No matter how wounded a wife seems one year, there's absolutely no change for the better next year. The occasion that was missed comes and goes again, the husband forgets, the wife is shattered, and life goes on.

The husband probably never even knows that it's taken a little bit out of the marriage. Don't make this mistake. Don't think that just because you don't care for any of the fuss, your wife doesn't either.

And be honest with yourself. Don't you really like it when your wife makes a big to-do about you on your birthday? Don't you enjoy the attention, being on center stage? Doesn't it feel good that you're remembered?

That goes double for your wife. She needs to feel that you share the attachment to the important times in your lives. She can't help feeling that among all of your triumphs, the greatest is your marriage. Your anniversary is important to her and she needs to know that it is meaningful to you.

Ditto for her birthday. Although women demonstrably out-live men, each birthday has a tendency to bother them more. You must be aware that certain birthdays are especially traumatic. Such milestones as 30, 35, and 40 years are times when your wife needs the assurance that she is still desirable to you. If you can't be bothered to remember, it's obvious to her that she's not only not special, but you don't even care about her.

Your wife needs something tangible from you to prove that you know about her feelings and care about her. It doesn't have to be very big or expensive as long as she knows you made the effort to select something for her and her alone. Some husbands make the mistake of turning this task over to a secretary because they know they are going to forget the dates, because they wouldn't have time to shop for anything even if they did remember, and they wouldn't know what she wanted in the first place. These husbands feel that if they let their secretaries handle it, the gifts will be purchased on time and their wives will get something useful. Of course, if the husband is not there when the present is opened and doesn't know what it is, his wife can throw him off balance; but that can be overcome. The fact is, however, the wife always knows when the secretary has bought the present. It's a puzzle how she knows, but she does and it hurts her. And while it's better than forgetting altogether, it still falls short of what should be.

Your doing the shopping, and thus remembering personally, is precisely what makes the occasion so special. Your taking time out of a hectic day gives greater meaning to it. The present may not be exactly what she would select if she had chosen herself, but she can tell that you put some thought and time into getting it for her. And if you'd been listening at home as you should have, she probably off-handedly told you what to get her. Even if you don't get a clue, chances are she's not pining for the same perfume that you gave her last year and at Christmas and at every other occasion for the past three years.

Use these tailor-made opportunities to strengthen your marriage, to be romantic, romantic *because* of her. Devise some way to remember, and don't let important dates slip past. Take the time to shop yourself. If you're truly close to her you will have an idea of the kinds of things she wants. It may not be a surprise but it's something she likes or needs. Or go with her to pick out the present. Use your anniversaries or birthdays for those intimate, romantic dinners or those one-night getaways.

As you become truly romantic, you'll be doing these things for yourself as much as for your wife. You'll find pleasure in planning and sharing these moments with a woman, a very unique woman who knows she is very special to you. You'll find that these rare times bring you closer and help you to appreciate each other. They let your wife know that she is all woman to you and that she's precious because of it. You'll start to understand what makes her tick and look under the surface to what she really is. You'll want to be tender and loving so she knows and feels it, and give her that gentle hug, soft pat, or loving touch to make it real.

Your wife deserves a romantic husband. Be one to deserve a super wife.

10

Getting the most out of a company marriage

IT'S NOT TOO HARD to find an opinion poll that supports your favorite theory these days. One of the more interesting polls around says that most successful men have the habit of kissing their wives as they leave for work each morning. It's an interesting study because it leads to the conclusion that success in business breeds an affectionate nature and vice versa. Fascinating speculation.

Well, we all should have learned long ago that the way to success in any job is through hard work. There may be some people who just happen to be in the right spot or who simply hang around for years and years until something falls in their laps, but for the most part those who are successful are so because of talent and hard work. Thus, if these people are successful because of their effort and time on the job, the fact that they have a close enough marriage to want to kiss their wives goodbye as they depart for the day's work is quite revealing. You can probably discount that it's done as a matter of rote. You don't have to be married very long to get out of the habit of little things like kissing your wife when you leave and return. And that's too bad because it's a good reminder that you are man and wife.

No, the good-morning kiss for these successful men means much more than a mere routine. The fact that they think of it in the first place shows the importance of marriage in their lives. This good-morning kiss is also an indication of the strength they receive from their marriages for doing the job. It demonstrates that vital businessmen are drawing support from their wives. It points up the growing realization of what a good, solid marriage can do for a man in his vocation.

This realization is not irrelevant. More and more busy, overworked, thinking couples are discovering that there is a basic deficiency in their marriage. They are looking at what they have and don't have, and are coming to the conclusion that there should be more to marriage. And what's really significant is their determination to do something about it. That's the wonderful thing about recognizing that a marriage is dying—it can then be salvaged so long as both husband and wife want it to be. The relationship can be revived if you are alert to what has been happening and dedicate yourselves to correcting it.

There's no question that it takes hard work and effort; what matters is that it can be done and should be done. And if it's not always easy to learn from your own experience, learn from that of others. Look at those who have taken marriage for granted, have ignored the signs of deterioration, have pursued success to the exclusion of all else including marriage. They end up constantly dissatisfied, always chasing, always missing what they were too busy for.

Instead, take your cue from the successful men who take the time to kiss their wives good-bye in the morning. Learn from those who work to have the kind of marriage that will contribute to their career while giving them things material success cannot offer. Find out what's really important in life before it's too late to enjoy it, too late to recapture what might have been.

And don't delude yourself as to how much time you have. Now's the time to stop and take stock. Your wife and family may not always be there when you decide it's time. Now is when you must take positive action to have the kind of marriage that will give you the best of both worlds.

You may shrug this off, feeling there's no reason to bother. You're a good provider and you have given your wife and family many more material things than you ever had. You feel justified in putting in the long hours, and if anything, you feel it's your wife who should be concerned about taking care of you. Of course, there may be some truth in this thinking; it's possible your wife isn't doing her share. But you stand to lose so much by not doing yours. You may think you are tough and can get along without anyone else, but consider the alternative.

Instead of drawing strength from wife and family, eventually there will come a time when the friction and unfulfilled demands will drain your strength. Instead of the warmth and comfort everyone needs, you'll find coldness and rejection. Instead of the joy of sharing with those you love, you will find the bitterness of loneliness and the shallowness of material accomplishment. Instead of the sustaining purpose that the family can represent, you'll begin to question its value.

These bleak possibilities are not wild conjectures intended to scare you into being a good husband. They are real examples of what has happened to many who were unwary and unconcerned. They show what life can come to if you cheat on your marriage. But, they can be prevented if you and your wife want to prevent them badly enough, if you are willing to put in your fair share of work.

Signs of Deterioration

Hopefully you've already taken the steps to determine the present status of your marriage and what you want it to be. You might even go back to what prompted your marriage and consider whether your expectations have been satisfied. Did it ever approach what you wanted? It's more than likely you can point to a time when marriage was the sparkling, all-encompassing highlight of your life. If it's lower on the totem pole now, analyze what happened. Trace the decline step by step without laying blame or finding fault. Stand up to your own shortcomings and the ways you contributed to the decline. It won't do any good if your ego doesn't allow honesty. When did you first perceive that your marriage was no longer quite so idyllic? Was it when you got the first big promotion and didn't have so much time to spend with your wife? Or was it when she got her first break on her job and no longer had quite as much time for you?

Maybe it declined a little further when you took up a hobby she wasn't interested in. Then there was the first baby, whom you dearly loved but who demanded so much of her time. Or was it just getting used to each other, and taking the other for granted in such things as sex? When was the first time you were "too tired"? When did other women seem more desirable than your wife? Or did you gradually drift apart, you with your interests and she with hers? Have you watched your marriage decline and not cared? Maybe it started when the kids stopped needing you and you lost that common ground.

If your marriage has begun to deteriorate, it's probably because of time pressures, taking each other for granted, and losing vital communication. What's important is where you are now. If your marriage has improved, continue to concentrate on the areas that have done you so much good. Be alert to signs that you're starting to drift apart. Once you suspect a problem, act to solve it right then. If you know you're having a problem, if things don't seem quite the same, look back to what's changed from the time when your marriage was better. Don't ignore signs of deterioration. Catch them early and they're that much easier to handle.

One-Sided Success

But there can be another side to the deterioration process: you spot it, and you try to rectify it, but your spouse simply does not or will not respond. Even though you realize your errors and try to do better, she doesn't seem to care. She doesn't want to communicate. She won't go through the bother of figuring out what's important and won't contribute when you talk about marriage goals. And as you look back at your drifting apart you come to the sad conclusion that while you were at fault, she was too, and maybe even more than you.

Now she doesn't seem to care one way or the other what you do. It almost seems as though the more you try to do right, the worse you make things. You can reach a point where her reaction begins to get to you and then things really get sour. Instead of love and support, you get griping and bitching, and it eventually affects your job performance.

This is a real dilemma and brings you face to face with a question that has a most unpleasant answer. Can a marriage be successful when there is only one-sided effort? The answer is no. This doesn't automatically mean a divorce or separation, but it does imply that your marriage is not going to be what it should or could be. It means that although you are going through the motions, you'll never close the gap. It means that you're going to have to face the question of whether it's worth perpetuating such a marriage. It means you're going to have to decide whether staying together for the kids is worth it to you and to them. It means you're going to have to face some very unpleasant alternatives.

In the old days it was much simpler because it was hard to get a divorce; people stayed in a marriage come hell or high water. Now divorce is an accepted practice. But it can be a nasty business, one to be avoided if at all possible. Too often couples divorce because they think it is an easy way out; not that they couldn't make it go, but they didn't want to put the effort into it. If this is your situation, don't make that mistake. Keep plugging and working and fighting to save your marriage. Do everything in your power to make it work. Analyze and probe and make a go of it, no matter the effort or swallowed pride. As long as just one spark is left, pull out all the stops to fan it to life.

But if it remains moribund then you must face the alternatives. The first is to accept the way life is and make whatever adjustments are necessary to keep it bearable. It's possible to be satisfied with just the facade of marriage, you going your way and she going hers. It could be pleasant enough even if there's no real sharing. But it could also be very unpleasant, with each of you making cutting remarks, with one fight after another.

Maybe there are children involved and you think you must

stay together for their sake no matter what you have to put up with. That's a noble gesture, but you must question what good you are really doing. Again, you should go to the furthest extreme, but you may only be kidding yourself about how healthy your marriage is for your children. When children are used as innocent pawns between warring factions, the good is questionable. If everything else is wrong, staying together for the kids probably is wrong too.

The other alternative, kids or not, is separation, official or otherwise. If you've done all you can to make the marriage go, this serious step must be considered. A decision requires a lot of careful thought. You must make a list of things such as who will live where, how much more money it will take, and how much there is to go around. You must also carefully weigh what it will do to the kids, what it will do to your lifestyle, how it will affect your children's emotions as well as your own.

All of these changes must be anticipated and measured against what you have now. As in evaluating the prospect of a job, the security of the known may outweigh the temptations of the unknown. The main thing is to give thorough thought to the present situation before you decide that it's hopeless. You shouldn't give up if there is any chance at all. Marriage is too precious to chuck just because there are some stormy moments, and often it can be saved if both partners are willing to make it work. But the key word is both. As much as you may want to try, you cannot do it all by yourself. When you realize that the effort is all one-sided you must squarely face the agonizing alternatives. Marriage is a two-way street—there can be no one-sided success.

Stick Together

By far the best solution is to make the marriage work. It's better for you, it's better for your wife, and it's better for your children. By so doing you'll gain a tremendous amount of emotional support that you can use as currency on the job. With all the work you put into making your family life better you'll get a return that cannot come to you in any other manner. Therefore, give of yourself.

Remember, however, you cannot be mechanical about giving. You may have to start that way if you've gone wayward in your heart, but try to make it a natural part of your personality. Going through the motions can help you get back into the swing of things, but it's only good for starters. You must consciously put more of yourself into your marriage if you're going to make it succeed.

That's where you get the real return. If all your efforts don't produce it you'd better look at yourself. Is it that you're not really trying, or are your feelings just not there anymore? Are you getting a response from your wife but you don't feel anything? Is the marriage better, but still not particularly satisfying? If you can't put your whole self into the marriage and get a corresponding return, you're either not giving enough or your relationship is too dead to revive. But if you cared enough to make the effort and you've kept trying, it's unlikely that it's dead. Don't give up on yourself too soon. Your approach may be mechanical and not very romantic or tender, but if you keep pushing the day will come when you feel it on the inside, where it really matters.

One good way to keep going even when you have doubts is to count your blessings. This is an old technique that many give lip service to but never really think seriously about. It can make a difference in your life if you pause occasionally to think about what you *do* have instead of what you do not. It's so easy in day-to-day living to take the good for granted and dwell on the not-so-good. No life or marriage is going to be without travail or shortcomings. No one is going to have completely smooth sailing and you shouldn't expect to. But people can get so wrapped up in the bad that they forget what a lot of good there is too.

See if you have this tendency. Are things really as bad between you and your wife as you make them out to be, or are you letting a few problems get in the way of appreciating how much good you have? It's not an uncommon characteristic, but one that can do much harm in your marriage if you let it. So don't. Evaluate your situation from the standpoint of what's in your pocket now. Don't be afraid your blessings will go away if you stop to count and enjoy them. On the contrary, it will make them that much more meaningful to you. Your family can make life fuller and richer only if you take the time to savor them. By concentrating on what you do have you'll be better equipped to overlook some of the deficiencies that your wife undoubtedly has—just as she will undoubtedly overlook some of your shortcomings.

Of course you can jump on mistakes and thrive on words better left unsaid. You can nurture resentment because she slighted your needs in order to satisfy some of her own. You can brood because she didn't exactly please you when you were out with the boss. You can rant and rave if she goes over the budget on account of something that seems totally unnecessary to you. All these things and many more will happen throughout your married life, but they're no more serious than you make them.

If you go through all the mechanical steps to have a good marriage only to spoil it by holding grudges or dwelling on mistakes and weaknesses, you've nobody to blame but yourself when your marriage is less than satisfactory. You must learn to overlook what you consider deficiencies or quirks of nature in your spouse. And you must recognize your own faults and work to overcome them. You must learn not to add to a bad situation and make it worse. What will you have gained if you destroy your wife for not being perfect?

Don't make the mistake of letting your marriage get away from you because you didn't realize how well off you were. Remember that the perfect marriage is less than perfect, but that you can begin to approach true perfection by going all out as a husband.

Always Changing

It helps to remember that a viable marriage is always changing because the partners are. This fact should be a significant consideration when counting your blessings. You are a different person because of marriage; you've experienced growth and development, and your expectations are greater too. One of the reasons you know there is more to enjoy in life is because your marriage gave you more.

Keep in mind, then, that you are not the same person you were before your marriage and are no longer used to the same things. When you feel you are not getting out of marriage what you should, consider that what you've gotten out already has made you more than you were. Before you get too taken with the idea that your share is disproportionate, look at your wife. How has she changed? What has that change meant for her personally? What has it allowed her to contribute? There's no way you can ignore her contributions when counting your blessings. What she has been giving is no doubt a large part of what the good things in your marriage are all about.

Take a long look at your wife now and the woman you took for your bride. She's much the same, but she is also different. Look at the strengths you know about now but hadn't uncovered then. Look at the weaknesses that you can accept now, but that you wanted to ignore back then. See the influence she has had on you. Even if you are the hardest driving man in the world, chances are that she's made a difference in you in many ways. Don't forget the little quirks that are all her own and that make her so endearing to you. While you're at it, don't forget the things that brought you together and make staying together worthwhile. Look past the purely physical reasons. It's nice to have someone to come home to, someone to cook and do laundry for you, someone to help raise your children and keep you warm at night. All of these are nice but they are just part of the total package. What really makes her valuable is the whole person, the one who appeals to you as no one else can.

If you and your wife haven't reached that point yet where you are true friends, you have much to anticipate in your marriage. If you once reached it but now seem to have lost it, then you know it's worth whatever it takes to regain it. One of the great aspects of suddenly seeing your wife as a friend is the new world that opens to you as she changes, as you both change. You have already been positively affected by the changes she has brought to you, and you may anticipate more and better things in the future.

Back to Basics

You can only appreciate your own metamorphosis if you remember that marriage can make two people as one and that this has happened to you. It may have been brief but it was real and it affected you. Now, even though you have been drawing apart, that close exposure remains an influence you cannot escape. Nor should you want to because it's through this sort of impact on your basic character that marriage makes you more of a person.

And although you both are continually changing to some extent, there is still much that is common. There is the need to have that one person totally yours; the need to give of yourself unselfishly; the need to have someone with whom to share your hopes and dreams and triumphs and disappointments. Marriage can mean having that special friend and an all-fulfilling lover rolled into one. These basics of marriage do not change even though you do.

That's why you should do all you can to have and keep a solid marriage. It sustains you at home and energizes you at work. The right marriage is one that complements you as a whole, even though you may have to struggle to get that out of it. And while you may think another route would be easier, it would also be less fulfilling to you personally. The good marriage that gives you such a full life is worth fighting for. Don't lose it through shortsightedness or laziness or stubbornness.

And don't forget the comforts to be found in a good marriage. You may or may not be at the point in life where the hard drive sets you back just a bit. True, some never lose their energy and you hear a lot about those who put in long hours forever. That's great for them, but for the majority of us there comes a time when we want to slow down.

A large part of the middle-age crisis that's being widely discussed today is more than just waking up to the finality of not being a superman; it's seeing what it takes to make it and realizing that the desire and energy to go after it are lost. No one is immune to this, and when that day comes it can be a crusher, prompting all kinds of irrational behavior.

If it comes to you, and chances are it will, it can be devastating. Even if you feel you have always been honest with yourself, there's always that little corner of hope that you will be the greatest at something someday or that your ship will finally come in. But the day of truth inevitably dawns and then you know that your dreams are never to be.

This may lie heavy on your heart, but it's not catastrophic. There will always be some sadness but there'll be less of it and it will be so much easier to accept if your marriage is solid, if your wife is there to share it with you. And it's not nearly the surprise for her that it is for you. Her pain will come from seeing you hurt, but she will not be disappointed in you. And that can and should be a great comfort. She's there because you are who you are, rather than because of any great deeds you may accomplish.

There's another way to view this coming to grips with reality. It's hard to see at first but it can bring new meaning and freedom to your marriage. As long as you think there's any chance at all for the brass ring there will be a temptation to cheat a little on your wife and children in favor of the job. If you have a marginal hour it will go to the company rather than to the home because you feel it will help your career. It's a great relief when that drive is past and you can go as you please without worrying about what it will do to your career. This doesn't mean that you quit giving your all to the job or never make that extra effort when it's called for. You still must do those things and you will want to. But acceptance of your status removes a great deal of pressure both at home and at work.

You can start relaxing at your job and as a result relax more easily at home. You can set aside time for your family without worrying. You can enjoy moments of pure inactivity which were unattainable before. You will never completely lose your dream, but you will appreciate more what you do have.

The Pure Pragmatics of Marriage

Having a good marriage is the smartest and most practical way to live. Even the most hardhearted realist who knows exactly where he's going needs wifely support. You'll have to admit that you're that much stronger with a live-in friend you can trust. There are times it helps to talk things out with someone whose loyalty to you is unquestioned. And it's a great boon to have a helper on the social front where you need to be active but hate to be bothered. For the pragmatic person, a marriage is worth working for just because of all the needs that are taken care of.

The pragmatic man appreciates the conveniences of marriage. He doesn't have the bother of such chores as washing clothes, cleaning the house, or cooking meals. And the realist should understand how much better it is to have sex with a known quantity than to look for, find, then fumble through the motions of sex with someone of undetermined compatability. This is wasted effort that can be eliminated by a loving wife.

All these points might sound crass—making marriage a matter of convenience rather than emotions, almost like a business arrangement. But it is all true to a certain extent. Marriage is much more than the physical attraction and sex that love is equated with today. Granted, physical attraction and sex play a large role in getting together in the first place. In the early days of marriage much of the pleasure comes from the physical contact and sexual relations. But as great as sex is, once you're past a certain point it is no longer all-encompassing.

That's why marriage must be a pragmatic arrangement and why matrimonial love is more than the common notion of love. Love between married partners transcends the physical aspects. It is the bond that truly holds the family together, but it's something that grows and develops and needs to be cultivated. When you work to have a strong marriage you build that kind of love. It may sound like a cold approach, but it's not. There must have been a basic feeling there to start with or you would not have been married, but if you let the fires cool, you not only have to regain what you had but surpass it.

In many ways, the old-time arranged marriages were very successful. They worked because the people involved came to have a deep love for each other through the desire and effort to make the marriage viable. They knew what they had to do. They knew they had no alternative but to spend their lifetime together, so they did what they had to, and dedicated themselves to building their love through marriage.

The easy divorce, as stated earlier, may well be the greatest mistake of our modern society. So many couples decide they can't make a go of it because of relatively insignificant problems. They could patch things up if they were willing, but it takes too much effort and work. They part friends, with no animosity, feeling it's better to go their separate ways even if there are children. It's such a shame because they are depriving themselves of so much. Furthermore, the chances are that they will go through life searching for marital happiness and never finding it. Hopefully more and more of us are beginning to realize how important marriage is. It's not a simple, short-term sexual convenience, but a deeper, long-term commitment that rewards us far beyond the effort put into it. Love is the crux of marriage but it takes a successful marriage to really know what love is all about.

Marriage and Job

True meaning in life can only come from your marriage and your vocation. They're what give the highs, lows, joys, and sorrows—what make it all worthwhile. Marriage and career can be in eternal conflict, or you can work to create a harmony between them that will give your life richness beyond any expectations. It doesn't come easy but requires giving of yourself, your time, and your love. You can't give up because the stakes are too high. We're talking about a lifetime of fulfillment versus a lifetime of emptiness. The great danger is that if you don't realize what it can be, you'll lose it by default. That's why you should sit down and figure out what's important in your life, never losing sight of what you are working for and why.

In the total scheme of things it is easy to forget how much more marriage can mean to you than the job. The tangible rewards and potential of the job are always visible. You can see where you are going and what you will earn. Neither where you are nor where you are going is always so clear in marriage, and it is easy to lose sight of motivation. But you can learn from others, and what more and more people are saying is that what makes success on the job worthwhile is having someone to share it with.

If you have someone to share it with, if you already have the potential for everyman's dream, go after it. Invest your time and effort in making what you have now as good as it can possibly be. Be realistic as you contrast what you want with what you have. Be honest in searching your soul to determine how you have affected the marriage, good or bad. Reaffirm your commitment to making your marriage a success, and at the same time reexamine your understanding of what success on the job is all about. The two are compatible and your goal should be success in both. Will you dare to have the kind of life you can and should have? It's there for the taking.

And if you're still not certain what marriage is all about, if you're still unsure what it is you are after, go back and read the text of your marriage ceremony. Dwell over each magic word and let the majesty of your vows speak to your heart. Renew your understanding and sense of purpose. It can be a union of lasting beauty, enduring above all else in your life. At the same time you can succeed in business with a strong marriage helping to sustain you. You can live the good life by making your marriage and career goals pertain to what's important to you and your wife.

The bedrock, the cohesive force, of our society is the family. It is one institution that must be preserved if we are to survive as a nation. The only way it can be preserved is by married couples working to make their marriages what they should be.

It all comes back to you. If you are willing to meet the challenge and to accept your responsibilities for making it happen, you can. If you appreciate what a wonderful, precious resource your wife is and let her know your feelings, she will be all that you want and more. If you're willing to invest yourself, the returns will come back to you, multiplied many times over.

You can succeed in marriage and business and join that group of elite achievers who happily kiss their wives each and every morning on the way to their satisfying and rewarding jobs.